Now Hear This!
LANGUAGE ARTS

Activities to Improve Language Arts and Listening Skills

WE'RE ALL EARS!

by Ann Richmond Fisher and Betsy Fisher

Illustrated by Mike Artell

Teaching & Learning Company

1204 Buchanan St., P.O. Box 10
Carthage, IL 62321-0010

Cover art © Corel Corporation

Designed by Teresa Brierton

Copyright © 1999, Teaching & Learning Company

ISBN No. 1-57310-180-X

Printing No. 987654321

Teaching & Learning Company
1204 Buchanan St., P.O. Box 10
Carthage, IL 62321-0010

This book belongs to

_____

Dedication

This book is dedicated to all our Irish friends, especially Rachel, Amy, Orla, Cleo, Abigail and JoyAnne.

Table of Contents

Dear Teacher or Parent,

This is a resource you'll turn to repeatedly as you practice language skills with your middle-grade students. This is really two books in one—a language arts book that contains skills ranging from punctuation to poetry and a listening book that stretches skills in hearing and following directions. As you use the activities in this book, you are building students' language and listening abilities simultaneously. There is no need to take time away from this important content area while you teach good listening habits!

Many important language skills are covered in this book. The lessons are arranged by general topics as listed in the table of contents. Topics include sentences, parts of speech, spelling, vocabulary, reference skills, creative writing and more. Specific skills covered in each lesson appear in the top corner of your page. Usually easier lessons are placed first in each section. It is suggested that you begin with easier lessons so that the students' focus will first be on listening. You may also want to repeat directions two or three times in the beginning. Eventually, you will be able to move on to harder skills with less teacher help. The wide range of activities will keep your students interested and listening!

This book is a complete resource which contains everything from pretests to a chart for recording students' progress. Lessons require little preparation on the part of the teacher. For many of the lessons, your students will need only a piece of paper and pencil. For others you will need to photocopy a reproducible page. Materials needed are always listed in the top corner of the lesson, so you can see what is needed at a glance. An answer key is provided in the back of the book which will help you check students' results quickly.

The page that follows, "How to Use This Book," contains more specific instructions on using special features of this book. It is our goal to provide appealing, helpful lessons for you, the classroom teacher, as you seek to train your students in language and listening!

Sincerely,

Ann & Betsy

Ann Richmond Fisher and Betsy Fisher

o_ to Use This oo_

To get maximum benefit from the various features of this book, use the suggestions that follow.

Warm-Ups: These are fun activities at the beginning of each section that will introduce students to the upcoming content area. The purpose of the warm-ups is not only to give students a sample of the work ahead but also to get students excited about it.

Pre/Posttests: These have been written to help the teacher evaluate student progress. The teacher should carefully preview the upcoming unit before administering the pretest. If some lessons are inappropriate for your class (i.e. too difficult or too easy), then there may also be inappropriate items on the pre/posttest. Feel free to use only the questions on the tests that correspond to lessons in the unit you will actually be using. Come up with your own number for the highest possible test score. Use the **Teacher Record Page** to record the date of each pretest, the number of items on the test and each student's score. After the class completes all appropriate lessons in the unit, administer the same test again, and record student scores for the posttest on the record page. At a glance you can see which students are not improving. Try to work with them individually or in small groups to diagnose any problems they may be having.

Lessons: Most lessons are written so that you can read them to an entire class while each student completes one page of work. You can then collect the work and evaluate it using the **Answer Key** in the back of the book, or students can check their own work as the entire class works through the correct solution together. **Important:** In each lesson students are instructed where to write their names on the paper. Make sure they wait and listen to these instructions. Also note that for some lessons, student outcomes can vary from the answers shown and still be acceptable.

Although the lessons can be administered in a traditional manner described above, some can also be adapted to other formats. A few ideas are listed below. Use your imagination and try other ideas of your own as well.

Cooperative Learning Groups: Some activities can be completed in pairs or small work groups. This requires students to agree on what they've heard and to work together on their outcomes. "Chart Challenge" (page 39), "Table Talk" (page 60), "Encyclopedia Enterprise" (page 64) and others are suited to this format.

Chalkboard Lessons: "Rewrites" (page 15), "Find the Nouns" (page 25), "Outline a Sandwich" (page 65) and many others written on plain paper can be done at the chalkboard. You may wish to have three or four students at the chalkboard while the rest work at their seats. This allows you to spot problems immediately. The chalkboard worker may be distracting to the others; students will need to listen and concentrate even harder.

Remind students that other answers may be possible, or they may be incorrect. Emphasize the need for each student to do his own best work.

Team Relays: For "NVA" (page 26), "From Adjective to Adverb" (page 36), "Spell Spot" (page 54) and others, try this. Divide the class into teams of four to six students each. Have one member from each team go to the board and solve one problem, have the second member of the team do the next one and so on. All along the way, the team needs to listen carefully to be sure instructions are followed. Allow one person from each team to have the opportunity to correct earlier mistakes.

Content Variations: For many lessons, the content can easily be changed while retaining the format and instructions. Such lessons include "Watermelon Words" (page 42), "Spell Check" (page 44) and "Guide Game" (page 58).

TLC10180 Copyright © Teaching & Learning Company, Carthage, IL 62321-0010

Teacher Record Page

		Pretest 1	Posttest 1	Pretest 2	Posttest 2	Pretest 3	Posttest 3	Pretest 4	Posttest 4	Pretest 5	Posttest 5	Pretest 6	Posttest 6
	Date												
Student Name	# possible												

Materials:
Reproducible on page 10
Pencil

Sentences

Write your name in the top right corner of your test paper. Throughout the exercises on this page, be sure to use correct punctuation and capitalization.

For the first three blanks, I will read you a group of words. If the words make a complete sentence, write a *C* in the blank. If the words make an incomplete one, write an *I.*

1. Three beautiful baby birds

2. Sarah read a book.

3. David's pet snake hid under the sofa.

For numbers 4 and 5, I will tell you one of the missing words. You need to fill in the rest.

4. A **declarative** sentence . . .

5. An **imperative** sentence . . .

Now look at the information in the box above numbers 6, 7 and 8. For these, I will read you a sentence. If the sentence I read you is a declarative one, put a number 1 in the blank on that line, and so on.

6. What a beautiful day this is!

7. How do you like your hot dogs?

8. Please pass the mustard.

For number 9, unscramble this group of words. Write two different sentences using every word.

9. do carnival a lot at to there is a

10. Listen to this declarative sentence, and then rewrite it as an interrogative one.
    Uncle Rob loves to write music.

For numbers 11 and 12, add a subject or a predicate that will make a complete sentence.

For numbers 13 and 14, draw a line between the complete subject and complete predicate. Underline the simple subject. Circle the simple predicate.

15. Now listen to this sentence which is written in inverted order. Rewrite it in the usual manner.
    In a cabin in the woods lived a hermit.

16. Listen to this sentence and rewrite it in inverted order.

    The tired campers crawled into their tent.

Sentences

1. _____   2. _____   3. _____

4. A _____ sentence makes a _____.

5. An _____ sentence gives a _____ or makes a

   _____.

| 1: declarative | 2: interrogatory | 3: imperative | 4: exclamatory |

6. _____   7. _____   8. _____

9. _____

   _____

10. _____

11. Two tiny twigs _____

12. _____ drank three gallons of water.

13. My favorite singer appeared in a local concert.

14. Three wealthy men purchased the castle.

15. _____

16. _____

Just a Thought

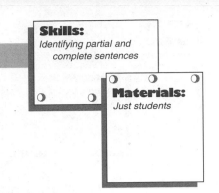

Use as a warm-up for Part 1.

You may already know that a sentence is a group of words that expresses a complete thought. Listen carefully to each group of words as I read it. If it is a complete sentence, raise your hand. If it is not, do nothing.

1. Most people enjoy pets.
2. The dog down the street
3. Pamela's cat ran up a tree.
4. Having the right pet food is important.
5. Barking loudly every night
6. Pets need a lot of tender loving care.
7. Going on walks and getting exercise
8. Five golden tropical fish
9. Hamsters and gerbils must have cages.
10. Bryce's favorite pet is a turtle.
11. A pony named Sugar
12. David's pet snake hid under the sofa.
13. Six homing pigeons were released this morning.
14. When the vet calls on Monday
15. Spiders are not very popular pets.

(Teacher: You may wish to go back over the incomplete sentences (2, 5, 7, 8, 11 and 14) orally and have students think of different ways they could be finished.)

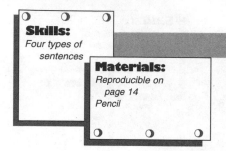

Skills:
Four types of
sentences

Materials:
Reproducible on
page 14
Pencil

Four Score

Write your name in the top right corner of your page. Then look at the numbered statements.

Fill in the blanks as I read to you.

1. A declarative sentence makes a statement.

2. An interrogative sentence asks a question.

3. An imperative sentence gives a command or makes a request.

4. An exclamatory sentence expresses sudden or strong feeling.

Next think about how you write a sentence. The first word of a sentence always begins with a capital letter. A sentence always ends with some kind of punctuation.

Declarative sentences and imperative sentences end with periods. Read the example sentences for numbers 1 and 3. Add a period to the end of each one.

Obviously, an interrogative sentence ends in a question mark, so put one after the second example.

Finally, an exclamatory sentence ends with an exclamation point. Put one by the fourth example.

Now you're ready to listen to some sentences. For each one that I read, you will need to write three things. First, write the beginning word of each sentence with a capital letter; then write the last word with the correct punctuation. Finally, write 1, 2, 3 or 4 to show which kind of sentence it is. The numbers 1 to 4 match the statements at the top of your page.

Four Score

Look at letter A and the three blanks. We will work through this one together to make sure you understand the directions.

Sentence A: Our family went on vacation last summer.

In the first blank, write the first word of the sentence using a capital letter. Do you remember what it was? The word was *our.* In the second blank, write the last word of the sentence, which was *summer.* What kind of punctuation will you use? Yes, a period.

What kind of sentence was this? Look at the four statements at the top of your page. This was a declarative sentence, so write the number 1 in the last blank. Do the remaining sentences in the same manner.

B. What a great time we had!

C. Please hand me the road map.

D. The Mackinac Bridge was our favorite spot.

E. How was the bridge built?

F. Roll down the window.

G. It certainly is hot in here!

H. When can you visit us?

I. Let us know when we should expect you.

J. We hope to drive to the west coast on our next trip.

Finally add up the numbers you wrote for sentences A-J. What was your score? You should have a total of 24.

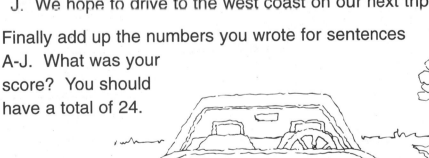

Four Score

Reproducible for use with pages 12 and 13.

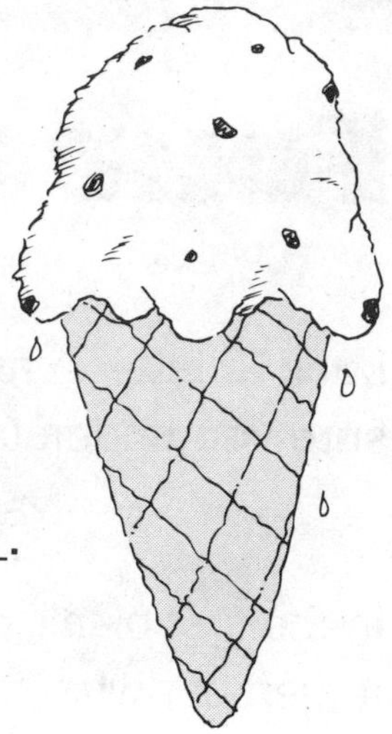

1. A **declarative** sentence makes a ______________________.

   Example: I like to eat ice cream

2. An **interrogative** sentence asks a ______________________.

   Example: What is your favorite flavor

3. An **imperative** sentence gives a ______________ or makes a

   ____________________.

   Example: Hand me the ice cream scoop, please

4. An **exclamatory** sentence expresses _________________ or _________________

   _________________.

   Example: This is so delicious

A. ______________________ ________________________ ___________

B. ______________________ ________________________ ___________

C. ______________________ ________________________ ___________

D. ______________________ ________________________ ___________

E. ______________________ ________________________ ___________

F. ______________________ ________________________ ___________

G. ______________________ ________________________ ___________

H. ______________________ ________________________ ___________

I. ______________________ ________________________ ___________

J. ______________________ ________________________ ___________

Total ___________

Rewrites

Skills:
Changing statements to
questions and
questions to
statements

Materials:
Lined paper
Pencil

Write your name in the top left corner of your page. Number 1 to 10, skipping a line between each number. I will read 10 sentences to you. If the sentence is a declarative sentence (one that makes a statement), rewrite it as an interrogative sentence (one that asks a question). If the sentence is an interrogative one, rewrite it as a declarative one.

For example, the sentence *Johnny can run fast* could be rewritten as *Can Johnny run fast?*

Be sure to use correct capitalization and punctuation.

1. The new song was a hit.

2. Will the singer go on tour?

3. She owns her own jet.

4 Her clothes are really wild.

5. Is her hair usually green?

6. My uncle writes songs.

7. One was recorded in a studio.

8. Uncle Rob sold his own tapes.

9. Will he become famous some day?

10. He won't let fame go to his head.

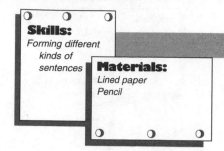

Skills:
Forming different kinds of sentences

Materials:
Lined paper
Pencil

Carnival Craze

Number from 1 to 7, skipping two lines between each number. Write your name in the top left corner of your page. For each line, I will read you a group of words which can be formed into a sensible sentence. Write two different sentences for each group of words. Remember the four different kinds of sentences. You may write interrogative, exclamatory and imperative sentences as well as the usual declarative one as long as you use every word that I give you.

(Teacher: You may wish to preview the spelling of carnival, a lot, relative and Ferris wheel and/or write them on the chalkboard.)

1. do carnival a lot at to there is a

2. games rides and find you can fun

3. booths clown and Ferris are wheels acts there also food

4. carnival favorite are apples food taffy a

5. you at meet friends your carnival the can and relatives.

6. displays there farm carnivals most at are

7. go fun carnivals to is to it

Skills:
Finding complete sentences

Materials:
Any story or reading book

Paragraph Punctuation

Here's a quick idea to see if your students are listening!

Choose a paragraph from a story or library book. Select one that contains at least four or more sentences. Read it aloud as if it had no punctuation. Ask your students to listen carefully and decide how many sentences it contains. Also, you may want to ask students to go to the board and have each one write one of the sentences with correct capitalization and punctuation.

Subject Search

Skills:
Identifying subjects and predicates

Materials:
Lined paper
Pencil

Every sentence has two main parts: the complete subject and the complete predicate. The complete subject is the part that tells whom or what the rest of the sentence is about. The complete predicate tells what the subject is or what the subject does or what happens to the subject.

Listen to find the subject of this sentence:

> The blue truck raced down the street.

Did you decide the complete subject is *the blue truck?* The rest of the sentence is the complete predicate.

Now number your paper from 1 to 10. Listen to each sentence and write just the complete subject of each one. A word of caution: The subject is not always at the beginning of the sentence.

1. Tiny grasshoppers covered the field.
2. The insects ate everything in sight.
3. Hopping and chirping, the green creatures ate contentedly.
4. Three sisters captured some of the grasshoppers.
5. Daily, the girls fed tiny insects to the grasshoppers.
6. Their entire family watched them grow.
7. After much discussion, the family members decided to release the grasshoppers.
8. When they were set free, the grateful grasshoppers appeared to be smiling.

For number 9, write your own complete sentence. Underline the complete subject. Write your name at number 10.

Optional Extra Activity for Older Students

Now go back over your first eight answers. Look for the most important word in each subject. In our example, *the blue truck,* the word *truck* is the most important. This is called the simple subject. Circle the simple subject in each sentence 1 through 9.

SUB- JECT!

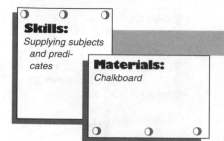

Skills:
Supplying subjects and predi-cates

Materials:
Chalkboard

Silly Subjects

(Teacher: Have three to five students at a time go to the chalkboard. They can simultaneously write their own responses. The rest of the class can then check their work for capitalization, punctuation, spelling, grammar and origi-nality.)

In this lesson, I will first read you just the subject of a sentence. You need to listen carefully and then write a predicate that will complete the sentence. Be sure to include the ending punctuation. You may be as silly (or serious) as you like, but be sure that you make a complete sentence.

1. The red and blue zebra
2. A martian made of marshmallows
3. The funky football
4. Seven slimy snakes
5. My fidgety frog
6. Twenty talking toasters

Now I will read to you just the predicate. It's your turn to write a subject. Remember to use capital letters when necessary.

7. zoomed along the clouds
8. tore up the book
9. scampers to the watering hole
10. swam his way to the beach
11. jetted over the road
12. will give a boring speech

18

Skills:
Finding simple subjects
and predicates

Materials:
Reproducible on
page 20

Two Parts

You may already know that every sentence has two parts: a subject and a predicate. The subject tells whom or what the sentence is about. The predicate tells what the subject is or does.

Look at the sentences on your worksheet. The first one has been divided for you between the subject and the predicate. Now read all the words in the subject. Which is the most important word? Underline it. This is the simple subject.

Now find the most important word in the predicate. It is called the simple predicate, and it is always a verb. Circle the simple predicate in the first sentence. Now let's check your work. You should have underlined *detective* and circled *solved.*

Next, look at sentences 2, 3 and 4. For each one, divide it between its subject and predicate. Underline the simple subject, and circle the simple predicate (or verb) as you did in number 1.

In numbers 5 through 10 you will see complete subjects. Underline the simple subject in each one. Then write your own complete predicate and circle your simple predicate (verb).

For number 11, write a complete sentence which will tell your teacher that this is your paper.

Two Parts

Reproducible for use with page 19.

1. The sly detective/solved a mystery.

2. Many students in my class praised his work.

3. They believed he was the best detective ever.

4. Disappearing ink proved to be the secret.

5. My lovely pet canary _____.

6. The static on the telephone line _____.

7. Her energetic grandmother _____.

8. A brilliant scientist _____.

9. My little baby brother _____.

10. A shiny black limousine _____.

11. _____.

Inverted Insight

Skills:
Changing the order of subjects and predicates

Materials:
Lined paper
Pencil

As you know, a sentence expresses a complete thought. It has a subject and a predicate. Sometimes to make our writing more interesting, we may want to put the predicate before the subject in a sentence. This is called inverted order. Listen to these two sentences:

A. The river flowed beside the woods.

B. Beside the woods flowed the river.

Even though the order of the words is different, in each sentence the subject and the predicate are the same. What are they? Yes, *the river* is the subject and the other words are the predicate.

Now write your name in the top right corner of your page. Number from 1 to 6. I will read six sentences to you. If the sentence is in the usual order, with its subject first, write a *U* on the line. If the sentence is in inverted order, write an *I* on the line.

1. Into the store walked a young boy.
2. He bought chocolate cookies.
3. Mother followed him home.
4. On the porch waiting for them sat Grandmother.
5. Next to Grandmother sat Lucy.
6. The children changed into their pajamas.

SUREFIRE WAY TO INVERT ALL SUBJECTS AND PREDICATES.

Now number from 7 to 12, skipping a line between numbers. This time I will read you a sentence where the subject comes first. You need to rewrite each one in inverted order, so listen carefully.

7. An old man lived in the woods.
8. A frisky squirrel scampered in the oak tree.
9. Dozens of geese flew overhead.
10. Two brown bears lurked nearby.

Finally, write two new sentences of your own. Write one in the usual order and one in inverted order.

Materials:
Lined paper
Pencil

Nouns, Verbs, Adjectives and Adverbs

Write your name in the top right corner of your page. Number the lines as we work, matching the number of the question that I read.

1. Listen to this sentence, and write every noun that I read on the first line of your page.

   In Ireland there are a lot of castles, green hills and sheep.

2. On line 2, write three proper nouns for the common noun *city.*

3. On line 3, write a common noun for the word *Smith.*

4 On line 4, tell if the word *grade* is usually used as a noun, verb or adjective.

5. Listen to the sentence I will read for number 5. Write each plural noun that you hear, and beside it write the singular form of the same noun.

   Most babies love mashed potatoes.

For the next two sentences, tell if the word *round* is used as a noun, verb or adjective.

6. We sang a song in a round.

7. Please round your numbers to the nearest hundred.

For the next three sentences, write first the helping verb or verbs and then the main verb on your line.

8. The teacher has helped us a great deal.

9. A lot of people should be attending the play.

10. The movie was not shown as scheduled.

BAAA...

YEAH, RIGHT...

Nouns, Verbs, Adjectives and Adverbs

11. Tell if the verb used in this sentence is in past, present or future tense.

    The farmer feeds the chickens every day.

12. On line 12, write these four words: *choose, chose, named, crown*. Underline the word that best completes this sentence:

    At the end of the contest, Maria was ____ the winner.

    Draw a line through the word that can be used as a noun or a verb.

13. On line 13, write the adverbs that can be formed from these two adjectives: *rare, easy*.

14. Listen to this sentence. Write the adverb that you hear on line 14, and next to it write two more adverbs that have opposite meanings.

    Orchestra music played softly in the background.

15. On line 15, write three adverbs to tell how, when and where a child might play.

16. On line 16, write a sentence about your teacher. Use two or more adverbs to describe how he or she does something. Underline the adverbs.

Skills:
Sentence building with parts of speech

Materials:
Just students

Add-Ons

Use as a warm-up for Part 2.

Conduct this activity orally with the class divided into groups of approximately five students each. Review the definitions of *nouns, verbs, adjectives* and *adverbs*. Then ask each group to write their own sentences, with each student adding one word to the group sentence. (You may want one person in each group to record the final sentences to share later with the class.) Follow these steps:

1. Student 1 chooses a noun. (For example: chickens)

2. Student 2 chooses an action verb to go with the noun. (Chickens clucked.)

3. Student 3 adds an adjective. (Seven chickens clucked.)

4. Student 4 adds another adjective. (Seven noisy chickens clucked.)

5. Student 5 adds an adverb. (Seven noisy chickens clucked endlessly.)

6. If there are extra students in the group, instruct them to add another adjective and/or adverb. (Seven noisy red chickens clucked loudly and endlessly.)

Then rotate parts and write more sentences.

Skills:
Listing proper nouns

Materials:
Paper
Pencil

A to Z

Use as a warm-up for Part 2.

Work with the class as a whole, or divide into small groups. Make one list for the group. See how quickly they can list a proper noun beginning with every letter of the alphabet. Have the rest of the group check the list for correct spelling and capitalization.

You can repeat this exercise using other categories such as action verbs, adjectives or adverbs.

Find the Nouns

Skills:
Identifying nouns in sentences

Materials:
Lined paper
Pencil

Write your name in the top right corner of your page. Number from 1 to 15. I will read 15 sentences to you. For each one, write just the nouns that you hear me read. Each sentence will contain at least one noun, and some contain many nouns, so listen carefully! Spell each word the best you can. *(Note: You may wish to write the word "Ireland" on the board for students.)*

1. Betsy lives in Ireland.

2. Betsy lives with her mom, dad, brother and pet turtle.

3. In Ireland there are a lot of castles, green hills and sheep.

4. Betsy and her family like visiting the castles.

5. The sheep are used for wool and meat.

6. Dublin is the capital of Ireland.

7. Beautiful crystal is made in Ireland.

8. Factories give tours so people can watch the glass being made.

9. Betsy goes to school and learns the Irish language.

10. Math, reading, science and history are some of her other subjects.

11. Betsy takes her own lunch to school.

12. Friends like to play tag during recess.

13. The class has over 30 students.

14. Her teacher is very helpful.

15. Betsy is looking forward to a visit from her relatives.

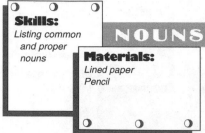

Skills:
Listing common and proper nouns

Materials:
Lined paper
Pencil

Proper Brainstorming

Number your paper from 1 to 12. For each numbered line, I will give you a common noun. You need to quickly list three proper nouns that fit the category. For example, if I said "state," you could write *Michigan, New York* and *Alaska.* Remember to use capital letters where needed and to do your best to spell all words correctly.

1. city
2. pet
3. relative
4. country
5. street
6. holiday
7. month
8. girl
9. boy
10. day
11. landmark
12. adult

Now number from 13 to 20. Next I will read a proper noun for each number, and you need to write a common noun that describes it on the correct line. Will you use capital letters on this part?

13. Asia
14. "Jingle Bells"
15. Chevrolet
16. Jefferson
17. Mt. Everest
18. Smith
19. French
20. Sacramento

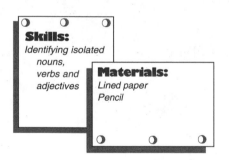

Skills:
Identifying isolated nouns, verbs and adjectives

Materials:
Lined paper
Pencil

WHEW!

Number your paper from 1 to 16. For each number, I will read one word. Write *N* if it is a noun, *V* if it is a verb or *A* if it is an adjective. Sometimes, the word I read can be used in more ways than one. For example, *table* can be a piece of furniture (a noun) or something that is done in a business meeting when a proposal is postponed (a verb). In this case, you should write both *N* and *V* on your paper.

1. white
2. brook
3. sing
4. granola
5. shuttle
6. nine
7. read
8. ruby
9. shovel
10. pew
11. watch
12. eat
13. grade
14. mink
15. lucky
16. Write your name by number 16.

Plurals, Please!

Skills:
Identifying and spelling irregular plural and singular nouns

Materials:
Lined paper
Pencil

Write your name in the top left corner of your page. Then number from 1 to 12. For each number, I will read a sentence that contains at least one plural noun. Write the plural or plurals that you hear. Next to each one, also write the singular form of the same noun. Do your best to spell each word correctly.

1. Several mice squeaked inside the old barn.

2. Last night, two calves were born on the farm.

3. Mrs. Rivera used peaches and cherries for her pie filling.

4. The flags of three countries flew over the building.

5. Bert dropped his car keys into a huge pile of leaves.

6. The thieves were caught red-handed because their feet became stuck in wet cement.

7. A pair of oxen lumbered down the path.

8. Three deer and two moose ran across the field.

9. My shoes became covered in mud as I walked out to see the sheep.

10. Both men and women like to receive flowers.

11. Most babies love mashed potatoes.

12. Three wives worked together to bake 20 loaves of bread for the bake sale.

KIND OF MUDDY, HUH?

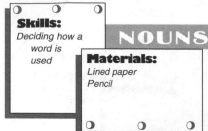

Skills:
Deciding how a word is used

Materials:
Lined paper
Pencil

NOUNS, VERBS, ADJECTIVES AND ADVERBS

Multiple Meanings

Number your paper from 1 to 12. I will tell you a key word for each sentence that I read to you. You need to listen carefully to decide how the key word is used in each sentence. Write the word *noun*, *verb* or *adjective* to tell how it is used in each sentence.

1. **PICTURE**   I can just picture our family enjoying the beach!
2. **PICTURE**   We found Dad's picture in an old yearbook.
3. **CHECK**   The check was written for five hundred dollars.
4. **CHECK**   Please check the bread in the oven.
5. **LIGHT**   Let's take our light jackets on the picnic.
6. **LIGHT**   Tonight we'll light the fire in the fireplace.
7. **LIGHT**   Please turn off the light before you leave.
8. **ROUND**   The antique oak table was round.
9. **ROUND**   The song we sang was a round.
10. **ROUND**   Now round each number to the nearest ten.
11. **WATER**   I would like a nice, cold glass of water.
12. **WATER**   Because we've had no rain, I need to water my plants.

Now number from 13 to 15.

For number 13, write a sentence of your own using *TIE* as a verb.

For number 14, write a sentence using *TIE* as a noun.

Write your name next to number 15.

Skills:
Finding helping verbs
and main verbs

Materials:
Lined paper
Pencil

Varied Verbs

Listen for the verb in these sentences:

> Keith plays the piano.
> Keith was playing the piano.
> Keith has been playing the piano.

In the first sentence, what was the verb? Yes, it was *plays.* The verb is an action verb of one word. In the other two sentences, however, the verb is more than one word: *was playing* and *has been playing.* These groups of words are called helping verbs.

Some words that can be helping verbs are *am, is, are, be, been, was, were, will, have, has* and *had.* There are others as well. They are called helping verbs when the verb appears with a main verb. Listen to this sentence:

> Bryce will find the answer.

What is the entire verb phrase? (*will find*) What is the helping verb? (*will*) What is the main verb? (*find*)

Now write your name in the top left corner of your page. Number from 1 to 12. Divide the lines into two columns. Label the first column *Helping* and the second *Main.* Listen to each sentence as I read it. Write each helping verb in the first column and each main verb in the second column. Remember, there can be more than one helping verb in a sentence.

1. Our class has performed several plays.
2. Recently, we were choosing our next one.
3. Soon we will be rehearsing the play.
4. Every day we will memorize a few lines.
5. The teacher has helped us a great deal.
6. He has been making posters.
7. Parents have been sewing costumes.
8. A printing company will provide tickets.
9. Other students can help, too.
10. Props will be provided by several families.
11. A lot of people should be attending our performances.
12. This year's play will surpass all others!

TWO BEES
OR NOT
TWO BEES...

Skills:
Finding verb phrases that are separated by other words

Materials:
Lined paper
Pencil

Divided Phrases

(Teacher: Use this lesson after "Varied Verbs" on page 29.)

You may remember that if verbs are made up of more than one word, we say the verb is a verb phrase. For example, in the sentence: *Fred is driving tomorrow*, the verb phrase is *is driving.*

If we change the sentence to an interrogative one (a question), the verb phrase will be interrupted by the subject. Here are two examples:

> Is Fred driving tomorrow?
> When is Fred driving?

Verb phrases can also be interrupted by other words. Listen to these examples:

> Kathy was not riding the horse.
> Kathy has already ridden the horse.

In the first, the verb phrase *was riding* is separated by *not.*

In the second, the verb phrase *has ridden* is interrupted by *already.*

Words like *not, already, never, now, often, seldom* and *yet* are adverbs. They are NOT VERBS.

Divided Phrases

Number your paper from 1 to 12. On each line first write any helping verbs you hear in the sentence I read. Then write the main verb. Do not write any words that are not verbs.

1. I have often visited the Queen.

2. Will she remember me?

3 My neighbor has not met Her Majesty.

4. The movie was not shown as scheduled.

5. We are still waiting to see it.

6. My little brother has never seen a musical.

7. Have our cousins left for vacation?

8. Did they take their sleeping bags?

9. They will probably return on Saturday?

10. Hopefully, you can now find verbs easily.

On line 11 write your own sentence containing a verb phrase. Underline the helping verb(s). Circle the main verb.

Write your name on line 12.

Materials:
*Three cardboard signs
labeled **past, present**
and **future***
Scrap paper
Pencil

Tense Times

Verbs show whether sentences refer to the present, past or future time. In grammar this time is called the *tense.* I will read three sentences to you. Listen to tell the verb tense of each one.

> I sing. (present tense)
> I sang. (past tense)
> I will sing. (future tense)

Notice that the form of the verb changes with its tense. Sometimes, for instance, you must add an *s* or an *ed* at the end. Sometimes you have to simply change the spelling.

Raise your hand if you can tell me the past and future tense of these present tense verbs: wish (wished, will wish); give (gave, will give); paste (pasted, will paste); eat (ate, will eat); know (knew, will know).

Now on your scrap paper write three good sentences. Write one in present tense, one in past tense and one in future tense.

*(Teacher: Select three students to go to the front of the room, and give each one a sign labeled **Past, Present** or **Future** to hold.)*

When I call your name, read any one of our sentences aloud. The rest of the class needs to listen and decide first of all if it is a complete sentence. If it is not a complete sentence, we will discuss how to fix it and then move on to another student.

If it is a sentence, then the three people in the front must decide which tense is used in your sentence. The person with the correct sign should hold it up. Then the class will decide if the correct tense was chosen. If so, I will call on another student to read a sentence. If not, the person holding the sign may change places with the student who wrote the sentence.

Skills:
Choosing the correct
verb

Materials:
Reproducible on
page 34
Pencil

Verb Choice

Write your name in the top left corner of your page. Your worksheet contains 10 rows of words, most of which are verbs. For each line, I will read you a sentence, leaving out one word. Select the word from your page that works best in each sentence. Remember to choose an answer that makes the tense of the rest of the sentence. Circle your answer.

1. Did you _____ the question?

2. My mom carefully _____ the peaches.

3. Strong winds _____ down the banner.

4. Dad _____ nearly every day.

5. The school choir has _____ at the program.

6. At the end of the contest, Maria was _____ the winner.

7. Have you _____ your new skateboard?

8. I _____ my marble under my bed.

9. Who can _____ faster, John or Di?

10. Anthony has _____ all of his dinner.

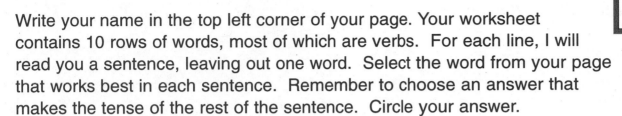

PICK A VERB...
ANY VERB...

Optional Additional Activity

Let's go back over your worksheet and look at the rows of words again. I will give you special instructions for each row, and I'll be skipping around, so listen carefully.

11. In row 3, put an X on the word that isn't a verb.

12. In row 6, underline the word that can be used as a verb or a noun.

13. In row 8, underline the present tense verb.

14. In row 9, draw a line through any past tense verbs.

15. In rows 1 and 4, put an X on the word that isn't a verb.

16. In row 7, underline the present tense verbs.

17. In row 5, draw a small circle above the two words that are forms of the same verb.

18. Pick one unmarked verb in rows 2 and 10. Use each one correctly in a separate sentence. Write your sentences at the bottom of your page.

Verb Choice

Reproducible for use with page 33.

1. heard   understand   simple   tried

2. wash   cooking   eat   peeled

3. blue   blown   blew   torn

4. exercises   listen   jump   almost

5. play   sung   appear   sing

6. choose   chose   named   crown

7. ride   trade   finds   used

8. seen   found   disappeared   hides

9. speaks   swam   run   talked

10. eaten   finish   devours   cook

COOL! THIS VERB CHOICE HAS SOME CHOICE VERBS.

Skills:
Creative thinking with adjective and alliteration

Materials:
Lined paper
Pencil

Menu Mania

1. Write your name in the top right corner of your page.

2. Pick any letter of the alphabet that is the first letter of a lot of interesting words. Write this letter on the first line of your paper.

3. Now make up a new restaurant. Choose a name that uses words beginning with your letter. For example, if you chose the letter C, you might name your restaurant *Carl's Cozy Cafe.* Write the name of your restaurant on the second line.

4. Use the rest of the page to make a menu. Draw the menu's outline and divide it into four sections for appetizers, beverages, main courses and desserts. If you want to add other categories, make extra sections accordingly.

5. Now add the names of foods to your menu using these two guidelines:
   1) Use at least one adjective in the name of each food.
   2) Use as many words beginning with your chosen letter as possible.
   For our example with the letter C, you could write under *Main Course* a food called *Crunchy Chicken and Corn Casserole.*

6. Double-check your menu for correct spelling. Underline every adjective you find.

(Teacher: If desired, have students copy menus onto colored paper, decorate and display in the classroom.)

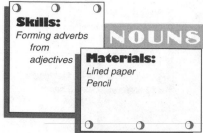

Skills:
Forming adverbs from adjectives

Materials:
Lined paper
Pencil

From Adjective to Adverb

Many adverbs tell how something is done. These adverbs are often formed by adding *ly* to adjectives. In this sentence: The puppy sadly walked away, the adverb *sadly* was made by adding *ly* to the adjective *sad.*

Note: For adjectives ending in *y*, the *y* is changed to *i* before adding *ly* as when *happy* is changed to *happily.*

Now number your paper from 1 to 15. I will read an adjective to you for each number. You need to change each one to an adverb and write the new word on your paper.

1. warm	4. sure	7. sleepy	10. rare	13. easy
2. usual	5. hungry	8. common	11. thirsty	14. shabby
3. real	6. first	9. greedy	12. honest	15. brave

Write your name at the bottom of your page.

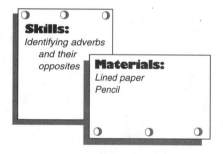

Skills:
Identifying adverbs and their opposites

Materials:
Lined paper
Pencil

Opposite Adverbs

Write your name in the top right corner of your page and number from 1 to 8. Listen to each sentence as I read it. Find the adverb in each one and write it on the numbered line. Next to the adverb, write two more adverbs that are opposite in meaning.

1. The panicked driver angrily honked his horn.

2. Quietly, the kitten crept out the door.

3. The final student anxiously turned in her exam paper.

4. Orchestra music played peacefully in the background.

5. My little brother puts his toys away carelessly.

6. Our new teacher awkwardly called out our names.

7. We politely refused to answer the caller's questions.

8. Often we have ice cream for dessert.

Skills:
Writing sentences with adjectives and adverbs

Materials:
Reproducible on page 38
Pencil

Sales Talk

Write your name at the top of your page, and then look at the picture on your worksheet. I am going to ask you to write several sentences in the blanks below about the picture. Remember to use complete sentences with correct punctuation.

1. On line 1 write a sentence about the used car salesman. Use at least two adjectives to describe him. Underline your adjectives.

2. On line 2 write a sentence about the used cars, using at least two adjectives. Underline the adjectives.

3. On line 3 write a sentence about the customers, using at least three adjectives to describe them. Underline the adjectives.

4. On line 4 write a sentence about the mechanic. Use at least two adverbs to tell how or when he works. Circle the adverbs.

5. On line 5 write a sentence about the dog. Use at least two adverbs to tell how or when he barks. Circle the adverbs.

6. On line 6 write another sentence about the salesman. Use two or more adverbs to describe how he does something. Circle the adverbs.

7. On line 7 write a final sentence of your choice, using at least one adjective and one adverb. Underline the adjective and circle the adverb.

Sales Talk

Reproducible for use with page 37.

1. _____

2. _____

3. _____

4. _____

5. _____

6. _____

7. _____

Chart Challenge

Skills:
Listing adverbs

Materials:
Blank paper
Pencil

Adverbs are used to describe, or modify, verbs. They can tell *where*, *how* or *when* something is done. Listen to these three sentences:

Sally runs there.

Sally runs quickly.

Sally runs now!

It is easy to find the adverb in each one, isn't it? In the first sentence, *there* tells where Sally ran. In the second sentence, *quickly* tells how she ran, and in the last one, *now* tells when she ran.

Now, along the left edge of your chart spell the word *ADVERBS* going down, with one letter on each line.

Next, fill in each space in your chart with an adverb that begins with a letter on the left and modifies the verb above it. For example, if you chose the verb *builds*, your adverb for the letter *A* could be *accurately*. Try to fill in the entire chart without using an adverb more than once.

Under the chart write this sentence:

I completed my work _____.

Fill in the blank with an appropriate adverb.

(Teacher: If desired, allow students to exchange charts and check one another's work. If some blanks were left in the charts, allow the partner to try to fill them in. If there are still blanks, allow the pair of students to consult a dictionary for possible solutions. Additionally, you could encourage a composite classroom list. This list could be posted for future references.)

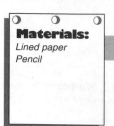
Spelling and Vocabulary

Write your name in the top right corner of your test paper. Number your lines from 1 to 25. On each line you will write either a set of letters that I will read to you or the answer to a set of instructions. Listen carefully as there are many different sets of directions.

1. Write the word *watermelon* on the first line of your page. Using only the letters in this word, write a five-letter word meaning "a citrus fruit" on the same line.

2. On line 2, write a four-letter word meaning "to wander aimlessly," using the letters from *watermelon*.

Write these two sentences correctly as I read them to you:

3. Their car is parked over there by the tree.

4. Who's going to tell me whose pencil this is?

For numbers 5 through 8, I will spell a word for you. If I spelled it properly, write *correct* on the line. If I misspelled it, write the correct spelling.

5. because

6. doesn't

7. niosy

8. tomorrow

For numbers 9 and 10, think of one more word that means the same as each set of words I will read to you.

9. remove, dismiss, expel

10. faltering, weak, timid

On line 11, write these six words: *tea, snow, some, storm, walk, where*. Match two pairs of these words to form two compound words. (Obviously, you will have two extra words.) Write these two new words on line 12. Circle the one that comes first in alphabetical order.

Spelling and Vocabulary

On line 13, write the letters E, I, L, P, R and S. Next to them, write a word that uses four of these letters that means "to go up." On line 14, write a word that uses all of the letters to spell the name for small tools used for gripping objects.

On line 15, write the letters S, D, E, G, I and T. Next to them, write a word that uses three letters and means "to bind with string or rope." On line 16, write a five-letter word that means "special plans for regulating what people eat and drink."

For 17 and 18, I will read you a set of three words. Write the word in each set that comes first in alphabetical order.

17. madhouse	madam	mad
18. bend	bench	beneath

For 19 and 20, write the word that comes last in alphabetical order.

19. gloss	globe	gloom
20. real	ready	reap

On line 21, write these letters: F L A T U S R U R R F Y. You will use some of these letters to spell words that match the clue I read you. There will be extra letters. You will not need to change the order of the letters to form the words.

22. a sudden gust of wind

23. the top layer of earth containing grass and roots

On line 24, write these letters: T A S B A F E R K

On line 25, write the longest word you can think of using as many of these letters as possible.

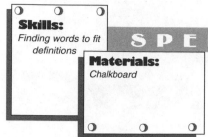
Watermelon Words

Use as a warm-up for Part 3.

*(Teacher: Write the word **watermelon** on the chalkboard. There are several different ways you could conduct this lesson. Have students raise their hand when they know the answer, write it on their own paper or have a team relay with one student at the board from each of three to four teams. Award a point to the first team to write the correct word.)*

I will give you a definition, and you are to spell a word that fits the definition using only the letters in *watermelon*. I will also tell you how many letters are in each word. For example, if I said, "a four-letter word that means the opposite of *cool*," your answer would be *warm*.

1. 4 letters: to change from a solid to a liquid

2. 4 letters: a spool on which fishing line or wire is wound

3. 5 letters: citrus fruit

4. 4 letters: a story

5. 4 letters: a long, slender creeping animal

6. 3 letters: tiny

7. 4 letters: to wander aimlessly

8. 4 letters: crippled

9. 5 letters: the main house on a large estate

10. 5 letters: a unit to measure length

11. 4 letters: food served at eating time

12. 5 letters: happening after the expected time

*(Teacher: If desired, have students find more words in **watermelon** and make up their own clues to read to the class.)*

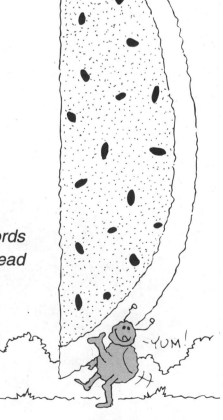

~YUM!

Skills:
Homonyms
Taking dictation

Materials:
Lined paper
Pencil

Dictation Duty

Write your name in the top right corner of your page. Number from 1 to 12, skipping a line between each number. I will read you 12 sentences. Listen carefully and write each sentence in its entirety on your paper. Pay special attention to the words that I emphasize.

1. It has been <u>quite</u> some time since the room was so <u>quiet</u>.

2. <u>Their</u> car is parked over <u>there</u> by the tree.

3. The boy <u>threw</u> the ball <u>through</u> the window.

4. In the <u>past</u>, an army <u>passed</u> by its house.

5. <u>Our</u> pets <u>are</u> ready to eat.

6. The <u>whole</u> gang helped dig the <u>hole.</u>

7. If <u>you're</u> going away, be sure to take <u>your</u> hat.

8. Giving everyone one <u>piece</u> of candy kept <u>peace</u> in the family.

9. <u>It's</u> time for the cat to have <u>its</u> milk.

10. Step on the <u>brake</u> before you <u>break</u> something.

11. Three boys went <u>to</u> the zoo, and <u>two</u> girls went <u>too.</u>

12. <u>Who's</u> going to tell me <u>whose</u> pencil this is?

Skills:
Spelling commonly
misspelled
words

Materials:
Lined paper
Pencil

Spell Check

Write your name in the top left corner and number your paper from 1 to 20. For each number I will say a word, and then I will spell it. If I've spelled it correctly, write the word *correct* by the number. If I have misspelled it, spell it correctly by the number.

1. already
2. because
3. beleive
4. busness
5. carefull
6. Christmas
7. diffrent
8. dosen't
9. fourteen
10. friend

11. heavy
12. kichen
13. meant
14. niosy
15. receive
16. scisors
17. seperate
18. studying
19. tomorow
20. Wednesday

(Teacher: You can adapt any of your regular spelling words to this format, and cover any number of words at one time.)

Synonym Search

Skills:
Synonyms

Materials:
*Reproducible on
page 46
Pencil*

Write your name in the top left corner of your worksheet. You will see numbered rows of words on your page. For each line, I will read you three words that are very similar in meaning. Circle the word in each row that means the same as the ones I read.

1. goods, effects, merchandise

2. glow, blaze, gleam

3. ransack, plunder, rummage

4. remove, dismiss, expel

5. blend, unify, integrate

6. unstained, pure, immaculate

7. sullen, stern, glum

8. vigilant, watchful, sleepless

9. hinder, obstruct, impede

10. joyful, lively, jovial

11. penniless, needy, indigent

12. faltering, weak, timid

13. recall, recollect, reminisce

In the last two blanks, write two sentences of your own. Use one of the words you circled in each sentence.

Reproducible for use with page 45.

1. property   program   progress

2. radical   brush   radiate

3. reek   return   raid

4. waver   oust   welcome

5. merge   split   dissolve

6. mobile   spotless   fair

7. grim   cordial   flashy

8. drowsy   helpful   alert

9. prevent   favor   tolerate

10. calm   jolly   dismal

11. powerful   poor   fine

12. feeble   generous   noble

13. forget   remember   return

14. _____

15. _____

SEARCHING FOR SYNONYMS??? NEXT EXIT Fresh synonyms... cheap

Compound Caper

Skills:
Compound words
Alphabetical order

Materials:
Lined paper
Pencil

Write your name in the top left corner of your page. Make two long folds to divide your paper into three columns. Label them A, B and C.

In column A, write the 20 words I will read you, with one word on each line. The words are: *pop, rattle, side, some, apple, snow, tea, them, under, step, door, sports, table, green, team, text, after, air, drum, ear.*

In column B, write the next 20 words. Again, write one word on each line. The words are: *ground, bell, where, spoon, child, work, muff, corn, walk, craft, house, noon, wear, snake, storm, stick, sauce, book, selves, cloth.*

Now draw lines to connect one word from column A to one word in column B so that a compound word is formed. Write each new word that you make in column C. These can be in any order. Try to make matches so that you use every word in both columns exactly once.

Finally, number your new compound words in alphabetical order. Put a 1 after the word that comes first, a 2 after the word that comes second and so on.

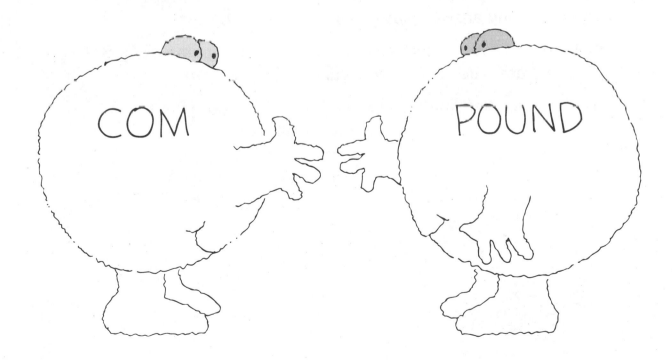

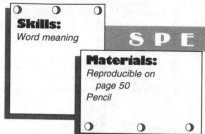

Skills:
Word meaning

Materials:
Reproducible on
    page 50
Pencil

S P E L L I N G   A N D   V O C A B U L A R Y

Puzzling Pyramids

Write your name in the top right corner of your page. You should see four pyramids on your page, each with an empty box above it. I will read you a set of letters which you need to write in the box. Then you will use only those letters to spell words in the pyramids.

1. In the box above the first pyramid, write the letters E, I, L, P, R and S. Now use one letter to spell the top word in the pyramid. It is a pronoun that refers to me. What word will you write? Yes, the word *I.* For the second word in the pyramid, use the letter I plus one more letter from the box to spell a word that is a form of the verb *be.* What did you write? Yes, the word *is* is correct. For the third word, use the letters I and S plus one more to spell a respectful term when addressing a man. Did you write the word *sir*? Continue in this manner, adding one letter from the box for each row in the pyramid. Here are the rest of the clues:

    Four-letter word: to go up
    Five-letter word: places where ships load and unload
    Six-letter word: small tool for gripping objects

Complete the remaining three pyramids the same way. Always use letters from the preceding answer, plus one more from the box.

2. In the box above the second pyramid, write the letters A, P, R, S, T and Y. Use these clues to complete each row:

    One-letter word: an indefinite article or "noun marker"
    Two-letter word: father
    Three-letter word: to strike lightly
    Four-letter word: time gone by
    Five-letter word: a narrow strip of leather
    Six-letter word: a pie, tart or similar dessert

Puzzling Pyramids

3. In the box above the third pyramid, write the letters S, D, E, G, I and T. Use these clues to complete each row:

One-letter word: personal pronoun
Two-letter word: in tag, the person who must catch another player
Three-letter word: to bind with string or rope
Four-letter word: the rise and fall of the surface of the ocean
Five-letter word: special plans for regulating what people eat and drink
Six-letter word: to change food into a form the body can use

4. In the box above the fourth pyramid, write the letters A, B, D, E, H, R and T. Use these clues:

One-letter word: one or each
Two-letter word: a preposition meaning "on, in, near or by"
Three-letter word: a rodent
Four-letter word: to rip apart
Five-letter word: the muscular organ that pumps blood
Six-letter word: fine string used in sewing
Seven-letter: width

Optional Bonus Activity

Write one of these words and subtract one letter at a time, so that the remaining letters can be rearranged to spell a new sensible word. See if you can "shrink" your word to a one-letter word.

Vinegar   leather   predict   patterns

Puzzling Pyramids

Reproducible for use with pages 48 and 49.

1.

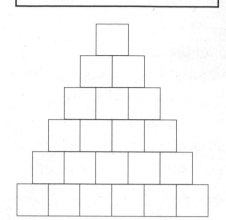

2.

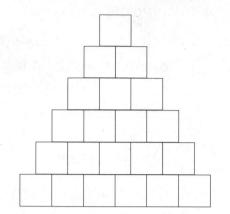

3.

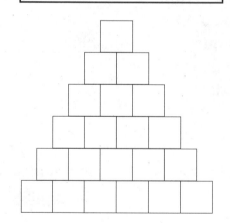

4.

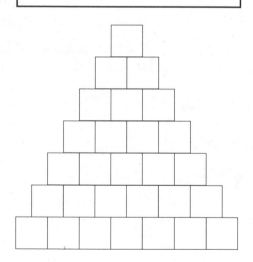

THESE PYRAMID PUZZLES ARE POSITIVELY PERPLEXING!

Skills:
Spelling
Alphabetical order

Materials:
Lined paper
Pencil

First or Last?

Write your name in the top right corner of your page. Number from 1 to 15. For the first part of the activity I will read you three words, all beginning with the same letter of the alphabet. Think carefully about how each word is spelled, and choose the one that comes *first* in alphabetical order. Write that word on your paper.

1. corn, chew, chart
2. dry, ditch, down
3. point, push, press
4. shell, salt, scale
5. the, three, this
6. flash, flame, flag
7. grace, grab, grade
8. bound, bottom, border

For the rest of this activity, I want you to write the word that comes *last* in the alphabet.

9. velvet, vent, vegetable
10. help, heat, heavy
11. number, nugget, nurse
12. lonely, loud, loom
13. jiffy, jiggle, jigsaw
14. workout, word, work
15. mink, minute, minus

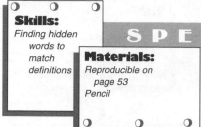

Skills:
Finding hidden words to match definitions

Materials:
Reproducible on page 53
Pencil

Letter Lines

Write your name in the top right corner of your page. On your paper you will see several rows of letters. You will use some of these letters to spell words that match the clue I will read you. There will be extra letters in every row. You will not need to change the order of the letters to form the words.

1. In row A, circle five letters that appear in order from left to right which spell a word that means "to fill with great surprise or wonder." Then using all new letters, find a four-letter word that names a precious metal. Write this word on the line. (Hint: You will not use the first two letters for either of the words.)

2. In row B, circle seven letters that a spell a word meaning "to answer or reply." Then use three new letters to spell a word that means "a large tank". Write the word on the line.

3. In row C, circle five letters that spell a word meaning "to change." Next, use different letters to spell another five-letter word, this time one that means "to wear away." Write the word in the blank.

4. In row D, circle six letters to spell a word meaning "the usual practice or habit." Then find a three-letter word, using all new letters, that means "to disturb or annoy." Write the word in the blank.

5. In row E, circle six letters to spell a word meaning "an official order or decision." Next, find five new letters that spell a word for "a sudden feeling of sickness or faintness." Write the word in the blank.

6. In row F, circle five letters that spell a word meaning "quickness of motion." Then use six new letters to spell a word meaning "not wasteful." Write this word in the blank.

7. In row G, circle five letters that spell a word meaning "serious" or "important." Next find four new letters that spell a word meaning "sharp." Write this word in the blank.

8. In row H, circle five letters that spell a word meaning "faithful." Then find four new letters that spell a word meaning "keen enjoyment."

CIRCLES ARE MY FAVORITE SHAPE!

Letter Lines

Reproducible for use with page 52.

A. T R A G M A C O Z L D E   _____

B. R O V E S A P T O N Y D   _____

C. A M E L R O T D E R E N   _____

D. C L U V E S H O T O X M   _____

E. Q U A D E C L R E T E M   _____

F. C H A F R U S T E G A L   _____

G. G A K R A T H E V E E N   _____

H. C L O Z E Y A S T O L D

Spell Spot

Number your paper from 1 to 10, skipping a line between numbers. For each line I will read you a set of eight to 10 letters. Write them on the lines as I read them. Then quickly spell the longest word you can think of using those letters. Use both lines to jot down as many ideas as you can think of in the seconds that I will give you.

(Teacher: Give students 20 to 40 seconds, as needed, for each set of letters. You may choose to tell the students that it is possible to spell a common word using all the letters in each line.)

1. l a p s o r e n
2. d a b e c e f k
3. m o p e l i t i
4. e s p i l p y r
5. p o t e s a n o
6. c l i t s h o k m
7. t a s b a f e r k
8. d a c u s q i n k
9. o d o f o r u n p s
10. l e t c h o t l a b

Write your name at the bottom of your page. Go back over each set of words. Double-check your spelling, and make sure you used the correct letters. Circle your longest word for each line. Give yourself one point for each letter in each word. Find your total score and write it at the bottom of your page. Compare it with your classmates'.

Materials:
*Reproducible on
page 56
Pencil*

Reference Skills

Use your dictionary to find words that fit these descriptions:

1. A two-word entry beginning with C

2. A word beginning with R that can be used as a noun or verb

Look at the pairs of guide words shown under blanks 1 and 2. I will read you three words beginning with the same letter. Write the letter in the blank that is beside the pair of words that would be on the same page in the dictionary as the word I read.

3. paper   4. panel   5. par

In the first set of blanks at number 6, write these four words: *cola, cold, coin, coil*. Now rewrite these same words in alphabetical order in the second set of blanks.

7. At number 7 you will see four headings. Decide which one would make the most sense for a book title. Write it with correct capitalization on the top blank. Then write the three other headings as main topics in the blanks numbered I, II and III. Try to put them in the order that makes the most sense, and use capital letters where they are needed.

Look at the list of three parts of a book. I will read you some descriptions. In the numbered blanks, write the letter or letters for the book part I am describing.

8. It is arranged alphabetically.

9. It gives pronunciations of words.

10. It lists books, magazines and other sources of information.

In the box you will see part of an index from a book about the Pacific Ocean. Use it to answer questions 11, 12 and 13.

11. How many main topics are shown in this part of the index?

12. On what pages would you find information about the California Pacific Coast?

13. Suppose the book also includes a topic called "Freshwater fish."

    Where would this appear in the index?

14. At number 14 you will see part of a set of encyclopedias. The beginning letters of words included in each volume are shown on the spine. Circle the number of the volume containing the entry *Jamaica*. Put an X on the number of the volume where you would find *candles*. Underline the number of the volume where you would find *cyclones*.

15. Write your name in the bottom right corner of your page.

Reference Skills

1. _____   2. _____

A. pan-panther   B. pantry-paradise   C. paradox-pardon

3. _____   4. _____   5. _____

6. _____   _____

   _____   _____

   _____   _____

   _____   _____

7. _____

   I. _____   Edison's Early Inventions

   II. _____   Edison's Childhood

   III. _____   Thomas Edison, the Great Inventor

                                  Edison's Many Patents

   D. Bibliography   E. Index   F. Glossary

8. _____   9. _____   10. _____

11. _____

12. _____

13. _____

14.

1	2	3	4
A-Co	Cr-E	F-G	H-K

Area, 1-5
   depth, 3
   surface area 2, 4-5

Coast, 20-43
   Asian, 30-38
   Australian, 39-43
   North American, 20-26
   South American, 26-29

Skills:
Dictionary skills

Materials:
Set of classroom
dictionaries
Chalkboard

Scavenger Hunt

We're going on a scavenger hunt through the dictionary. Listen carefully as I call out each "clue." Then look through your dictionary. When you have found an answer, raise your hand. When I call on you, be ready to share your answer. I will write several correct answers for each clue on the board.

1. A four-syllable word that begins with N

2. A word that comes alphabetically between *juggle* and *jumble*

3. A two-word entry that begins with W

4. Two words that begin with double e.

5. A word beginning with B that can be used either as a noun or verb

6. Any word with a usage traced back to the 1600s

7. Any word with 10 or more definitions

8. Three compound words or phrases containing *white*

9. Two words that come between *zest* and *zinnia*

10. Any word beginning with F that has a silent consonant

11. An O word that comes from middle English

12. A hyphenated word beginning with S

13. A word beginning with T that appears more than once as an entry word

14. A D word that contains the schwa sound

15. A word beginning with G that can be used either as a noun or an adjective

16. Any two-letter word that is new to you

Skills:
Using guide words

Materials:
Chalkboard
Paper
Pencil

Guide Game

(Teacher: Write these sets of guide words on the chalkboard:
A. glove-gout, B. grace-grate, C. grateful-grin, D. grinder-grub.)

Write your name in the top right corner of your page. Number your paper from 1 to 15. Now look at the pairs of words I have written on the board. Imagine that these are guide words from pages in a dictionary. Remember that guide words show the first and last words on the page and that all words listed there must come alphabetically in between the two guide words.

For each number on your page, I will call out a word. Think about how that word is spelled. Find the pair of guide words that would be on the same dictionary page as the word I've given you. Write the letter by those guide words on your paper. For example, if I said the word *gnat*, you would write A because *gnat* comes between *glove* and *gout* in alphabetical order.

1. grant	6. glow	11. grizzly
2. grip	7. grape	12. gold
3. green	8. grits	13. greasy
4. glue	9. graze	14. grand
5. groom	10. go	15. grim

I'M YOUR GUIDE WORD. FOLLOW ME AND YOU WON'T GET LOST.

GUIDE WORD

Alphabetical Antics

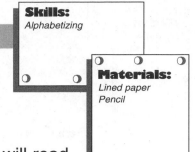

Skills:
Alphabetizing

Materials:
Lined paper
Pencil

Fold your paper in half vertically so that you have two columns. I will read you 20 words. Write them in the first column with one word on each line. Here are the words:

scar	scald
scanty	scan
scalp	scatterbrain
scarecrow	scarlet
scatter	scallop
scarf	scare
scamper	scat
scale	scant
scab	scarcely
scarce	scamp

Double-check your words to be sure you have the correct spellings.

(Teacher: At this point you may want to check students' spelling for some or all of the words.)

Now number your words from 1 to 20 in alphabetical order. Put a 1 by the word that would appear first in the dictionary and so on. Then recopy the words in alphabetical order in the second column.

THE SCARECROW IS SCARED BY THE SCAR ON THE SCATTERBRAIN'S SCANTY SCALP.

Skills:
Making a table of contents

Materials:
Lined paper
Pencil

Table Talk

For this lesson you will be making your own table of contents. Begin by writing your name in the top right corner of your page. Now turn your paper over. Use the back of your page to jot down your ideas, and then use the front to write your actual table.

Now think about a nonfiction book you could write about the state, province, county or community in which you live. Write down ideas for titles of your book.

Suppose your book will contain about 100 pages. Decide what major topics your book should include. Think of at least five or six chapter headings and write down these ideas. Then decide in what order they should appear and about how many pages should be in each chapter.

Now it's time to write your actual table of contents on the front of your paper. First write the title of your book. Center it on the top line of your page, using capital letters where appropriate.

Skip a line and then write your first chapter heading. Capitalize words as you would in a title. Show the page numbers for the first chapter.

Number each chapter heading with Roman numerals and skip a line between each chapter.

Continue in this manner until your table is complete. Double-check your spelling, capitalization and numbering.

Book Nook

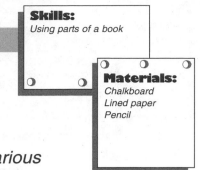

Skills:
Using parts of a book

Materials:
Chalkboard
Lined paper
Pencil

(Teacher: Before starting this lesson, review, if necessary, the various features of a book's introduction, table of contents, bibliography, glossary and index. Then put this list on the board: A. Introduction, B. Bibliography, C. Table of Contents, D. Index, E. Glossary.)

Number your paper from 1 to 12. I will read various descriptions to you. Decide which part (or parts) of a book I am describing and write the letter(s) in front of it on each line. For example, if the description was, "It gives definitions of words," you would write letter E for *glossary*.

1. It shows the page on which each chapter begins.

2. It may tell you the purpose of the book.

3. It lists books, magazines and other sources of information.

4. It is located before the first chapter of the book.

5. It is usually located near the end of the book.

6. It gives pronunciations of words.

7. It is arranged alphabetically.

8. It lists major topics by chapter.

9. It may be found more than once in the book.

10. It may have cross-references.

11. On this line, write the letters for each part in the order in which they would probably appear in a book, from beginning to end.

12. Write your name on number 12.

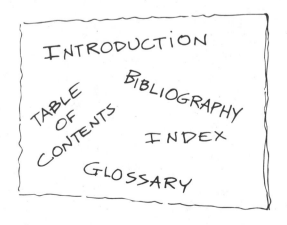

Skills:
Using an index

Materials:
Reproducible on
    page 63
Lined paper
Pencil

Index Info

For this lesson use the information on the worksheet. Write your answers on your own page of lined paper. First write your name in the top left corner and number from 1 to 10. Listen carefully to each question and write your answer on the numbered lines.

1. Which pages have information about the discovery of the Pacific Ocean?

2. On which pages could you find information about the Pacific Coast of Australia?

3. How many main topics are shown in this part of the index?

4. Suppose this book also includes a topic called "Ocean floor." Where would this topic appear in the index?

5. On which pages would you look for information about the places from which timber is shipped?

6. Which page would tell about the islands of Japan?

7. How many pages include information about shipping manufactured goods from Pacific ports?

8. In what two places could you possibly find out about oysters that are caught and shipped from the Pacific? (Write down the main topics or subtopics.)

9. Which main topic covers the most pages?

10. Think of another topic that might appear in this index.

Index Info

Reproducible for use with page 62.

This is part of the index in a book about the Pacific Ocean.

Area, 1-5
  depth, 3
  surface area 2, 4-5

Coast, 20-43
  Asian, 30-38
  Australian, 39-43
  North American, 20-26
  South American, 26-29

Commercial fishing, 67-81

Discovery of, 6-15, 110

Islands, 44-79
  Northern Hemisphere, 46-60
  Southern Hemisphere, 61-79

Map, 1, 6-7, 80-81

Ports, 45-49, 63-68, 78, 99
  cargo, 48-49, 67-68, 99, 103-106
    manufactured goods, 49, 68, 104-106
    natural resources, 48, 67, 99, 103-104
  volume, 50, 68, 99-100

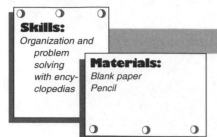

Skills:
Organization and
 problem
 solving
 with ency-
 clopedias

Materials:
Blank paper
Pencil

R E F E R E N C E   S K I L L S

Encyclopedia Enterprise

In this lesson you will be organizing your own set of encyclopedias. Listen carefully and follow each step in the directions.

1. Draw two large rectangles going across your paper, with one above another. Make each rectangle about 6" (15 cm) wide and 2" (5 cm) high so you will have room to write inside them.

2. Divide each large rectangle into eight equal parts by adding vertical lines in each row. These represent eight volumes of your encyclopedia set.

3. At the top of the spine of each book, write a number from 1 to 16. Start numbering at the top left.

4. Next decide how the alphabet is to be divided among the 16 books. I will read you several entry words along with the number of the book in which they appear. You should write down this information to help you divide the alphabet. (If you are not sure how to spell the entire word, write down the first two or three letters.)

Easter–3	gems–4	radiation–11	nylon–9
igloo–6	koalas–7	bullfrog–2	violin–15
penguins–10	X ray–16	glass–5	Saturn–12
bees–1	trucking–14	New Mexico–8	sun spots–13

5. Remember that words starting with the same letter can be divided between volumes according to their second letter. For instance, words beginning with AK could go in one book while words with AL could go in the following volume. Be sure as you are dividing the alphabet that no words will be left out.

6. Write your final letter groupings in the bottom portion of each spine.

7. Write your name above your set of encyclopedias.

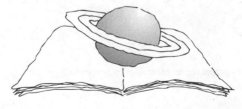

Skills:
Making an outline

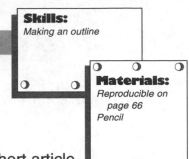

Materials:
Reproducible on
page 66
Pencil

Outline a Sandwich

Write your name in the top right corner of your page. I will read you a short article about peanut butter sandwiches. Your job is to listen carefully and complete an outline on your worksheet. The article has three main points which you should summarize at Roman numerals I, II and III. There will be subtopics under each main point as well. When you have heard the entire article, you can give it an appropriate title. Write the title, using correct capitalization, on the top blank of your page.

Article

If you ask a classroom full of American students what kind of sandwich is packed in their lunch, probably half of them would tell you they had a peanut butter sandwich. Peanut butter sandwiches continue to be a favorite with kids and parents alike because they are tasty, nutritious and economical. There are many variations of peanut butter sandwiches. In fact, each time you make one, you must make three choices.

First, you must select the bread you will use. Most people use store-bought bread, either white or whole wheat. Many kids prefer the taste of the plain, soft white bread. But many people also recognize the nutrition and fiber they gain from whole wheat bread.

Secondly, you must choose the type of peanut butter that you will put in your sandwich. Smooth peanut butter spreads easily. Crunchy peanut butter contains small bits of real peanuts which are fun to chew but can also get stuck in your teeth. Some people think that crunchy peanut butter has more flavor than smooth.

The third and final choice you must make when putting your sandwiches together is the type of additional spread you will use. The most popular choices are jelly, jam and honey. Jelly is made from only the juices of fruit so there are no bits of fruit in it. Cherry and grape are two favorite flavors of jelly. Jams contain pieces of real fruit, so many people prefer this spread. Strawberry jam is very popular in peanut butter sandwiches. Another good choice is honey. It is a natural sweetener and gives you quick energy.

The next time you're enjoying a peanut butter sandwich, think about all the choices that went into making the sandwich. You may decide to make different choices the next time and try a new variation on an old favorite.

Outline a Sandwich

Reproducible for use with page 65.

Title: _____

I. _____

    A. _____

    B. _____

II. _____

    A. _____

    B. _____

III. _____

    A. _____

    B. _____

    C. _____

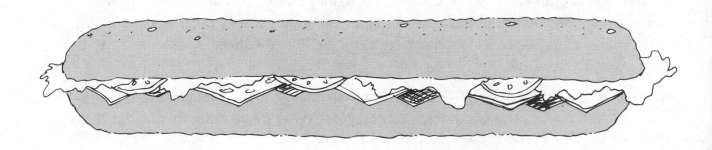

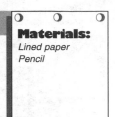

Materials:
Lined paper
Pencil

Creative Writing

1. First write a two-word poem. One word has to be a person's name; the other word has to rhyme with it. Notice, too, that if your "poem" is to make sense, it needs to contain a verb.

2. Now write a short story of one or two paragraphs about either a detective or a stubborn mule. Have the story take place in an office or a campground, and use these objects: a newspaper, magnifying glass, doll.

Write very briefly what these objects might do or say that only a person *really* could do.

3. a fish that doesn't want to be fed

4. a computer with problems that are difficult to solve

Listen very carefully to each partial saying as I read it to you. You need to write the words that I say, and then finish each proverb in your own new way.

5. The grass is always greener . . .

6. Two heads . . .

7. Choose a color. Think about how that color might taste. Think about how that color might feel. Write two lines of a nonrhyming poem about your color and these two senses.

8. Here is the beginning of a story. Use your own ideas to write a short ending to the story.

It was the most important invention of the decade, perhaps even of the century. Life would never be quite the same after the world was introduced to Miguel's discovery. After years of dashed hopes and broken dreams, Miguel knew that this time he had found the secret that would make him not only famous and rich, his name would become a household word; his Edison, Bell and Richmond . . .

Complete these limericks:

9. A lady who loved the bassoon
   Couldn't quite work out a tune . . .

10. A pilot who didn't like heights . . .

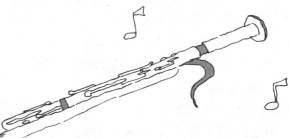

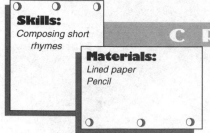

Skills:
Composing short
rhymes

Materials:
Lined paper
Pencil

The Name of the Game

Use this page as a warm-up for Part 5.

This is a short, fun lesson just to help you think of rhymes. I'll give you instructions for several different variations, all of which use the name of a person. You can write two or three examples of each kind of poem, and then try to write more of your own later.

A. First write a two-word poem. One word has to be a person's name; the other word has to rhyme with it. Notice, too, that if your "poem" is to make sense, it needs to contain a verb.

Examples: Jan can.
Scram, Sam!
Randy's handy.

Where is the verb in the third poem? Yes, the verb is *is*, contained in the contraction, *Randy's.*

B. Next try a three-word poem. Use a name, verb and another word that rhymes with the name.

Examples: Bryce is nice.
Kelly makes jelly.
Billie loves chili.

C. Now try a four-word poem where the second and fourth words rhyme and one of those words is a name.

Examples: Tell Ruth   Show Mabel   Give Greg
           the truth.   the table.   your leg.

Try to write many different examples for each pattern. Pick out three or four of your favorites to share with the class. Your class may choose to write a composite poem where each student writes about one name and all the lines are joined.

Skills:
Cooperative writing

Materials:
Chalkboard
Paper
Pencil

Random Writing

(Teacher: Divide students into groups of three or four each.)

In this activity your group will be given a character, a setting and a set of objects which you are to develop into a story. The information you are to use will be assigned to you in a random manner, so the stories you write may be quite surprising! Listen carefully so you will understand how to find your random information.

First, ask each member in your group to think of a number between 1 and 10. It's okay if two people pick the same number. Now find the total of these numbers. Then look at just the last digit of the total. That is your first key number. (For example, three people pick the numbers 3, 5 and 8. The total is 16. The last digit is 6, which is the first key number.)

Next, ask everyone to give the number of month of his or her birthday. Obviously, each number will be between 1 and 12. Again, find the total. Then use just the last digit. This is your second key number.

Finally, ask everyone to tell the day of the month of their birthday. (Each number will be between 1 and 31.) Again find the total, and use only the final digit. This is your third key number.

Now that your group has its three key numbers, you can tell me what those numbers are, and I will read the corresponding information that you are to use in your story. The first key number will tell you the identity of a character. The second will give the setting, and the third will give you a set of assorted items.

Characters

0. a talking rabbit
1. a king or queen
2. a detective
3. a gang of cowboys
4. a doctor
5. a family of 10 children
6. a well-known singer
7. a famous figure from the past
8. a computer whiz
9. a stubborn mule

Settings

0. a medieval castle
1. a tropical jungle
2. a summer cottage
3. inside a train
4. Hawaii
5. The Antarctic
6. a recording studio
7. a campground
8. a business office
9. a shopping center

HMM...

Random Writing

Objects

0. a map, a clock, a secret

1. a book, a chair, a bell

2. a treasure map, candy, a ring

3. a skateboard, a whistle, a bag

4. a jump rope, popcorn, a sock

5. a newspaper, a magnifying glass, a doll

6. a necklace, a telephone, a mug

7. a fireplace, a table, a safe

8. a portrait, a costume, a teddy bear

9. a handkerchief, a treasure chest, slippers

Now work with your group to make a truly creative story! You may use additional characters, settings and objects as well as those I have given you to use. Be sure to listen to everyone's ideas. Have someone write your completed story to share with the class.

(Teacher: There are many ways to vary this activity. By simply regrouping students, new sets of random information can be generated. You may also want to write your own list of settings, etc., or even have students come up with the lists.)

Personally Speaking

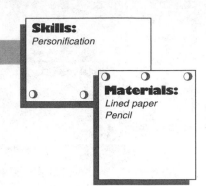

Skills:
Personification

Materials:
Lined paper
Pencil

Personification is a technique that writers use to give human qualities to non-human objects. For example, a tree might *sigh* in the wind, or a dog might *reply* to its owner. These are things only a person could actually do. But using personification in writing helps us communicate in an imaginative, clear way.

Now number your paper from 1 to 12, skipping a line between numbers. For each number, I will name an object and a situation for which you can use personification. Write very briefly what an object might do or say (that only a person really could do) in each instance.

1. a fish that doesn't want to be fed

2. a planet hidden by the sun

3. a chair that is supporting too much weight

4. an old trunk filled with momentos

5. a tropical island filled with colorful birds

6. some newspapers on their way to be recycled

7. a computer with problems that are difficult to solve

8. a kite that flies higher and higher

9. a book written by a famous mystery writer

10. stamps gathered for a child's prized collection

11. a CD of well-known songs

12. a jigsaw puzzle waiting to be put together

Now go back and choose your favorite from the list. Write an entire paragraph about the object and its "personality."

Proverbial Wisdom

Proverbs are short, wise sayings that apply to many different situations. They are usually very common and well-known. Number your paper from 1 to 15. Listen carefully to each partial saying as I read it to you. You need to write the words that I say, and then finish each proverb in your own new way.

For example, consider the proverb *Birds of a feather flock together.* You might rewrite it as *Birds of a feather make a nice pillow.* Make your proverbs as clever or as funny as you like.

1. When the cat's away . . .

2. Too many cooks . . .

3. All that glitters . . .

4. A fool and his money . . .

5. Every cloud . . .

6. The grass is always greener . . .

7. Two wrongs . . .

8. If the shoe fits . . .

9. Good fences . . .

10. A friend in need . . .

11. Two heads . . .

12. People who live in glass houses . . .

13. Half a loaf . . .

14. He who laughs last . . .

15. A bird in the hand . . .

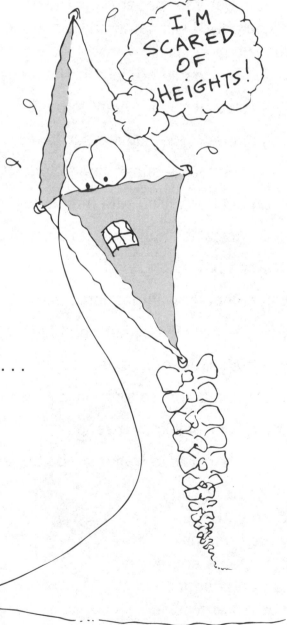

Skills:
Using sensory images

Materials:
Lined paper
Pencil

Colorful Poetry

Think about your favorite color. Jot down some ideas as we brainstorm together. You will use some of these ideas to write your own "color poem" at the end.

First, think of a lot of different items that are this color. List the obvious choices as well as the not-so obvious. For example, if your color were *red*, you might think of roses and valentines. But what about a crying baby or cherry pie?

Now think about smells. What would your color smell like? Is it a pleasant smell? Is it a strong or faint smell? Write down your ideas.

Thirdly, decide how your color sounds. Is it loud or soft? Again, using *red* as an example, it could sound like a fire engine siren!

Next, think about how your color tastes. Think of foods or temperatures or textures that you could feel with your mouth. Write down your ideas.

Finally, link your color word to an emotion. How does this color *feel?*

When you have thought about your color and all five senses, put your ideas into a simple, nonrhyming poem. You may want to use one line for each emotion. Here is a pattern you might choose to follow:

> Red
> It looks like glossy fingernail polish.
> It smells like a spicy cinnamon candle.
> It sounds like a fire alarm.
> It tastes like a crisp, crunchy apple.
> It feels ALIVE!

Be ready to share your poem with your classmates.

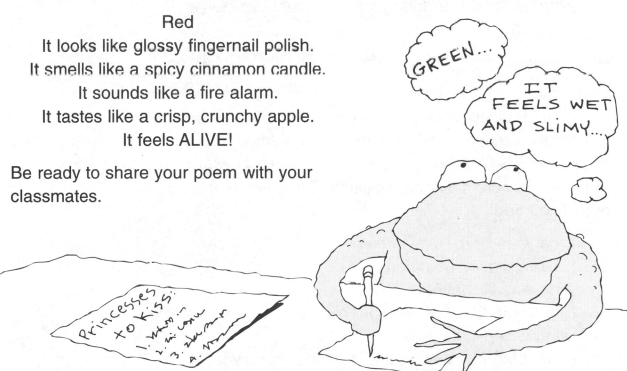

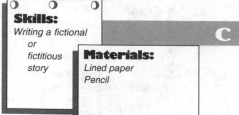

Skills:
Writing a fictional
or
fictitious
story

Materials:
Lined paper
Pencil

Story Starters

(Teacher: Instructions are written so that you may assign just one story at a time. However, you may choose to read several "starters" at one time and let students select one they wish to write about.)

I will read you the beginning of a fictional story. Listen carefully about what is in the "starter." Then I will ask you some questions to help you think about what is happening in the story and how you will complete it. Jot down your ideas, and then write the rest of the story.

Number 1

It was the third day of the third month in the year 2033. Anton had just been elected governor of the newest settlement on Mars. The election was a close contest, and Anton was eager to meet Troth, his defeated opponent, his friend again.

How should Anton seek to be friends?
Who was Troth?
What kind of people or creatures are Troth and Anton?
What kind of contest did Anton win to become elected?
What will his new duties be?
What is Mars like during the third month of the year?

Number 2

It was the most important invention of the decade, perhaps even of the century. Life would never be quite the same after the world was introduced to Bryce's discovery. After years of dashed hopes and broken dreams, Bryce knew that this time he had found the secret that would make him not only famous and rich, his name would become a household word; his Edison, Bell and Richmond . . .

What was Bryce's invention?
How would life be different?
Who was Richmond?
How could Bryce be so sure his invention was a success?
What was the secret?
How could he develop and promote his invention?

Story Starters

Number 3

Louise had always been a little different. Of course, there's nothing wrong with being different, but for once, Louise wished she could be like everyone else. She wished that the thing that made her different wasn't so obvious, so unusual. Yet in her moments of despair, she was always comforted by the wise words of her grandmother, words that Louise could still hear permanently recorded in her memory . . .

> What was Louise's "difference"?
> Why was it so obvious? So unusual?
> What were her grandmother's words?
> What happened to her grandmother?

Number 4

It was only four more days until the circus. Billboards were screaming the announcement. The fairgrounds were awaiting the crowds. Soon the bleachers would be sagging with the weight of the children, parents and grandparents who were even now buying their tickets and reserving their seats. No one could have anticipated the spectacular surprise that the ringmaster had in store for the quiet little town.

> What was the surprise?
> Who was the ringmaster?
> Where was this "quiet little town"?
> How would folks react to this surprise?
> What might happen in the next four days?

Number 5

"It must be that new cat food," thought Molly. "Why else would our little kitten have grown so much in just two weeks?"

"Maybe it's that blanket that Mom just bought for her little bed," suggested Mark.

"Whatever it is," replied Molly, "we must figure out how to stop it! Soon Kitty will be . . ."

> How big will Kitty be?
> Was it the cat food, the blanket or something else?
> What will happen next?

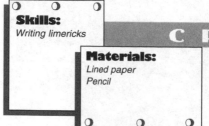

Skills:
Writing limericks

Materials:
Lined paper
Pencil

CREATIVE WRITING

Limerick Tricks

Limericks are well-known poems first written in and named after a city in Ireland by the same name. You may already know that limericks have five lines. The first, second and fifth lines are longer and rhyme with each other. Here is an example:

> A scholar, exceedingly smart
> Grew tired of learning and arts.
> So clever was he
> That he went on TV
> And made money just throwing darts!

Limericks are light, fun poems, but they can often be difficult to write. To help you get started, I will first read you some sample limericks that need only a final line. Listen carefully to the first four lines, and then write just the final line on your paper. Write two or three different endings for each one and see which one you like best. Compare your results with others'.

WHEW!

1. A chicken who laid a huge egg
   Tripped over it and broke her leg
   "Oh no," she exclaimed.
   "Please help me, I'm maimed!"

2. A gardener who didn't like dirt
   Always messed up his favorite shirt.
   "Finally," he said,
   "I'll work elsewhere instead."

3. A sharp-toothed hungry crocodile
   Who hadn't eaten for quite awhile
   Decided to fish
   For a nice tasty dish.

76

Limerick Tricks

Now I will read you some limericks that need the last *three* lines supplied. Write the first two lines as I read them. Then try to finish one or two of your choice.

4. A turkey who just lost his feathers
   Was dreading the wet, stormy weather

5. An anteater who didn't like ants
   Decided instead to chew plants

6. A lady who loved the bassoon
   Couldn't quite work out a tune

7. A burglar who wasn't so bright
   Couldn't learn how to keep out of sight

Finally, try these limericks where only the first line is supplied. Again, write the first line as I read it, and then try to complete two or more of your choice.

8. A leopard whose spots were missing

9. A mysterious young lad from Cork

10. A pilot who didn't like heights

11. A wealthy young widow from France

12. A child who liked to collect stamps

13. A patient who didn't like shots

14. An expert on high-speed racing

15. A spotted frog who'd lost his leap

Listening Comprehension

1. For the first blank, I will read you a series of words. Think of how each word is spelled, and write just the last letter of each word. These final letters will spell the hidden message.

    girl   ski   dress   chat   she   when

Next I will read you a brief article. Write the answers to the questions about the article in blanks 2 and 3.

Article: Do you know what language is the most widely spoken in the world? It is Chinese-Mandarin. About 960 million people speak Mandarin. This is twice the number of people who speak English, the second language on the list. Staying with English, the most common word in the language both in speaking and writing is *the*. The three most-used letters are *e, t* and *a*.

2. If 10 people speak English, how many people speak Mandarin?

3. What is the most common word in English?

4. Follow these instructions for the diagram at number 4:
    Add one more circle to each outer line of the shape. Write these words in the space outside the shape: *pin, per, car, cup, run.* Now write one letter in each circle so that the five words are spelled along the lines of the diagram. Place the letter C in the top circle to help you get started placing the words correctly. Write your name above the diagram.

For 5 and 6, I will read two statements to you. Decide what happened and write that under *Effect* on your paper. Write why it has happened under *Cause*.

5. Because the children were playing in poison ivy, they now have a rash.

6. I did not put enough stamps on the letter, so it was returned to me.

Look at the definitions written by number 7. I will read you a short portion of the story. Listen for words that fit the definitions on your page. Write a word from the story in the blank. You will have an extra definition.

Story: Crack! The capacious ship crashed into a floe in the Arctic Ocean. Immediately, Captain Jack appeared on deck, imploring his crew to give him a damage assessment.

8. Start with the word that appears at number 8 on your page. Follow the directions to rewrite the letters, one step at a time, to spell a new word.

    A. Replace the first vowel with an O.
    B. Insert a K between the third and fourth letters.
    C. Add a B at the beginning.
    D. Insert an O after the second vowel.
    E. Delete the second, fourth and seventh letters.

9. Find a sentence at number 9 that means the same as each set of sentences I will read. Write the letter by the correct sentence. (There is one extra.)

    A. My brother is hungry. Tell Sam. I am talking to you, Abraham.
    B. I am talking to you, Sam. Abraham is my brother. He is hungry.

Listening Comprehension

1. Hidden word: _____

2. _____

3. _____

4.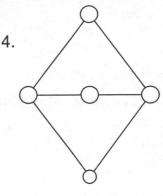

Effect   Cause

5. _____

6. _____

7. careless _____;   roomy and spacious _____;

   a piece of floating sea ice _____

8. READ

   A. _____

   B. _____

   C. _____

   D. _____

   E. _____

9. Sam, my brother Abraham is hungry. _____

   Abraham, my brother Sam is hungry. _____

   Abraham, tell Sam that my brother is hungry. _____

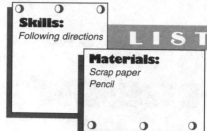

Skills:
Following directions

Materials:
Scrap paper
Pencil

LISTENING COMPREHENSION

Secret Codes

Use as a warm-up for Part 6.

In this activity I will explain briefly three different letter codes. Listen carefully to the directions so that you can solve each message. Take notes on your scratch paper to remind you how to solve each code.

Code 1

Each letter I will read to you needs to be replaced by the letter that comes three places after it in the alphabet. For example, if I say A, the correct letter is D. Letters at the end of the alphabet (X, Y, Z) are written as letters at the beginning (A, B, C respectively).

Now try to read this message: VLR EXSB QEB OFDEQ FABX.

Code 2

Each letter I will read to you should be replaced by the letter that comes two places before it in the alphabet. For example, if I say C, the correct letter is A. Letters at the beginning of the alphabet (A and B) are written as letters at the end of the alphabet (Y and Z).

Message: IQ DCEM VYQ URCEGU

Code 3

This code is quite different. I will read you a series of words. Think of how each word is spelled, and write down just the last letter of each word. These final letters will spell the hidden message.

Message: ZOOM COLA COOK THE PAPA IN SHE COW BRIM FREE IS GLASS IDEA RUG HOPE ALSO BLUFF CRY GO YOU TOWER HELLO SHOW MOON

Decide where to put spaces between words, and then write out the message correctly.

80

Listening for Lists

Skills:
Comprehension of facts
and details

Materials:
Lined paper
Pencil

Number your paper from 1 to 12. I will read you a brief article and then ask you several questions about it. Write just the answers on your numbered lines.

Article

Reference books provide a wealth of fascinating information. Almanacs, atlases, encyclopedias and dictionaries all contain a variety of facts that can be easily found. Did you know there are also many other types of reference books? A well-stocked library may contain dictionaries of abbreviations, phone directories for cities a thousand miles away, and books that can lead you to magazine articles about topics as specific as, "How to Care for Guinea Pigs."

One kind of reference book that has become very popular in recent years is a book of lists. In this book you can find the most common, most popular, best-selling, wealthiest, most frequent, longest, shortest, most expensive items, movie, book, dog breed, food or just about any other item. One such book is called *The Top 10 of Everything 1998,* published in London by Dorling Kindersley limited. The book contains over 200 pages of interesting lists on a wide range of topics. We will look at only a few.

Cats, Dogs and Other Pets

It may not surprise you to know that in the United States, cats are the most common type of pet, and dogs are second. But can you guess what the third most common pet is? They are parakeets!

JUST CALL ME. "MISTER POPULARITY."

Also in the U.S., the three most common dog breeds in order are Labrador Retrievers, Rottweilers and German Shepherds. Do you have a dog on this list?

One fact that is probably totally useless, but interesting nonetheless, is that the most popular name for a gold-fish in the United Kingdom is "Jaws." If you know any goldfish owners, you might like to take your own survey in this country.

Word Power

Do you know what language is the most widely spoken in the world? It is Chinese-Mandarin. About 960 million people speak Mandarin. This is twice the number of people who speak English, the second language on the list.

Staying with English, the most common word in the language both in speaking and writing is *the.* The three most-used letters are *e, t* and *a.*

Listening for Lists

Foods

Ireland has the highest average daily consumption of calories per person of any country in the world. Greece is second, Cyprus is third and the U.S. is fourth.

The most popular pasta product in the world is spaghetti, which accounts for 26% of the market.

Iceland leads the world in the amount of milk consumed per person, per year at over 306 pints per person. The U.S. falls way down the list at just 158 pints per person.

This is a sampling of the many varied facts found inside just this one book. The next time you're browsing in the library, don't forget to check into the fascinating facts found inside the huge variety of reference books.

Questions

1. List four different kinds of reference books.
2. The author mentioned a specific book of lists. Can you give its title?
3. What kind of pet is the most popular in the U.S.?
4. What are two of the most popular dog breeds in the U.S.?
5. What name was given as the most common goldfish name in the United Kingdom?
6. If 10 people speak English, about how many speak Mandarin?
7. What is the most common word in English?
8. List two of the three most common letters in English.
9. Which country consumes the highest number of calories?
10. Which country drinks the most milk per person per year?
11. What is the most popular form of pasta?
12. Write your name on line 12.

Diamond Diagram

Skills:
Drawing a diagram
Word play

Materials:
Blank paper
Pencil

1. Write your name in the top left corner of your paper.

2. Make a large diamond on your paper. Draw the outline lightly in pencil.

3. Now draw a vertical line to connect the top and bottom points of the diamond.

4. Draw a horizontal line to connect the left and right points of the diamond.

5. Next you need to add a number of circles to your diagram. Make each circle large enough so that you can print a letter of the alphabet inside it. Begin by making a circle at each point of the diamond. Also make a circle inside the shape where the vertical and horizontal lines cross. You should now have five circles. Make these five circles especially dark.

6. Now add three more circles to each outer line of the shape. Also add sets of three circles to each partial line inside the diamond. There should be nine circles on both the vertical and horizontal lines.

7. Now write these words in the space outside your diamond: *loose, petal, prior, enter, laser, primp, pearl* and *plate. (Teacher: You may wish to list these words on the board. The words* **pearl** *and* **petal** *can be switched.)* The five dark circles which you made first are where you will write the beginning and ending letters of the five-letter words.

8. To help you get started in placing the words correctly, write a P in the top circle of your diamond. Write an L in the dark circle inside the diamond.

9. Finally, fit in the other words to complete the diagram. Lightly cross off each word as you use it.

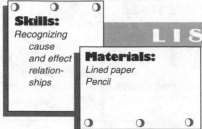

Skills:
Recognizing cause and effect relation- ships

Materials:
*Lined paper
Pencil*

LISTENING COMPREHENSION

Pause for a Cause

Write your name in the top right corner of your paper. Draw a line down the middle of your paper, dividing it into two columns. Label the first column with an *E* for "effect" and the second column with a *C* for "cause." Number from 1 to 10, skipping a line between numbers.

As I read each statement to you, decide what happened (the effect) and why it happened (the cause). Write a shortened version of each cause and effect on the numbered lines of your page. Notice that either the cause or the effect can come first in a sentence.

1. Because the children were playing in poison ivy, they now have a rash.

2. They used a special cream. As a result, the itching and swelling improved.

3. The rash was so uncomfortable that the children will be sure to stay away from poison ivy in the future.

4. I couldn't write to my pen pal because I lost her address.

5. Finally, she wrote to me, so then I was able to write to her.

6. I did not put enough stamps on the letter, so it was returned to me.

7. Because of the wet weather, the ball game was cancelled.

8. The team was very disappointed because they had been looking forward to the game.

9. I like my cereal to stay crisp, so I pour the milk and eat it right away.

10. Since Ralph prefers his cereal to be very soft, he adds milk and then waits 10 minutes before he eats his.

Captain Jack

Skills:
Finding word meaning from the context

Materials:
Reproducible on page 86
Pencils

Write your name in the top right corner of your page. I am going to read you part of a story about Captain Jack. As I read it, you may hear several words that are new to you. The meanings of 11 of these words are listed on your page. Listen carefully, and when you hear a word that matches one of the definitions on your page, write that word in the blank. Spell the words to the best of your ability. Take a minute to look over the definitions now before I read the story.

(Teacher: The vocabulary words students will need are underlined in the story for your convenience. You will probably want to read this aloud two or three times.)

Story

Crack! The capacious ship crashed into a floe in the Arctic Ocean. Immediately, Captain Jack appeared on deck, imploring his crew to give him a damage assessment. Since the ship was so large, apparently even this blow was not too detrimental. The crew breathed a collective sigh of relief.

Captain Jack calmly returned to his work, carefully studying his navigational charts. There was never anything haphazard about the way Captain Jack worked. To his crew he often seemed rather pompous, refusing to do any kind of menial work as long as there was someone else to do it for him. Occasionally, Jack had a hard time standing and sitting; then he complained of lumbago. His crew never knew if that was why he refused hard labor or if he just thought it was beneath him. His large girth proved that Captain Jack liked to eat, although one would not consider him to be glutton.

When you've finished with the definitions, draw a picture of how you think Captain Jack might look.

tain Jack

Reproducible for use with page 85.

1. something that causes damage _____

2. lowly; fit for servants _____

3. pain in the lower back _____

4. one who eats excessively _____

5. roomy and spacious _____

6. self-important _____

7. a piece of floating sea ice _____

8. as a group _____

9. the distance around an object _____

10. begging _____

11. careless _____

Soldier Salute

Skills:
Following directions

Materials:
Lined paper
Pencil

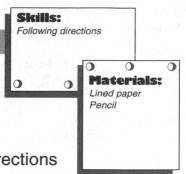

What do you call a quiet soldier? To solve this riddle, follow the directions very carefully as I read them to you.

1. Begin by printing these words on the first line of your paper: QUIET SOLDIER. Now ignore the space between words.

2. Rewrite the letters on a new line after each step of instructions. Add an L between the second and third vowels from the left.

3. Replace the R with a T.

4. Replace the third consonant from the right with an N.

5. Insert the letters GH immediately after the fifth vowel from the left.

6. Delete the third vowel from the right.

7. Replace the fourth consonant from the left with a K.

8. Insert an N between the fifth and sixth letters from the left.

9. Delete the second and sixth letters from the right.

10. Replace the first two letters with an S.

11. Rewrite the same letters, leaving a space after the sixth letter.

12. Write your name at the bottom of your paper.

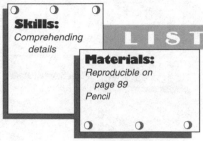

Skills:
Comprehending details

Materials:
Reproducible on page 89
Pencil

LISTENING COMPREHENSION

Turtle Tales

Write your name in the top right corner of your page. Then get ready to listen closely on this tricky activity! I am going to read you sets of simple sentences that can be combined into one longer, more interesting sentence. You need to decide which sentence on your worksheet means exactly the same as the set of sentences that I read to you.

For example, suppose I read these sentences:

My pet is a cat. Her name is Fluffy.

There are many ways these sentences could be combined. Here is one way:

My pet, Fluffy, is a cat.

I will read you a set of sentences. Write the number given with each set of sentences into the correct blank on your worksheet, the blank beside the sentence that has the same meaning.

Note: There are three extra sentences on your page.

1. Abraham is my pet turtle.
   He is very hungry.

2. Abraham is very hungry.
   My pet turtle is very hungry.

3. Abraham is my pet turtle.
   He likes to swim.
   Sam is my brother.
   He likes to swim, too.

4. Abraham likes to swim.
   Sam likes to swim.
   My brother likes to swim.

5. My brother is hungry.
   Tell Sam.
   I am talking to you, Abraham.

6. I am talking to you, Sam.
   Abraham is my brother.
   He is hungry.

7. Sam is my brother.
   He has a pet turtle.
   Abraham is the turtle's name.
   Abraham likes to swim.

8. Sam wants to stop swimming.
   Abraham wants to stop swimming, too.
   Sam wants to eat.
   Abraham wants to eat, too.

9. Abraham is my pet turtle.
   Abraham wants to stop swimming.
   He wants to eat.

Turtle Tales

Reproducible for use with page 88.

A. Sam, my brother Abraham is hungry. _____

B. Abraham, my brother Sam is hungry. _____

C. Abraham, tell Sam my brother is hungry. _____

D. Abraham and my pet turtle are both very hungry. _____

E. Abraham, my pet turtle, is very hungry. _____

F. My brother, Sam, has a pet turtle named Abraham who likes to swim. _____

G. Abraham, my pet turtle, and Sam, my brother, both like to swim. _____

H. Abraham, Sam, my brother, and my turtle all like to swim. _____

I. Abraham, Sam and my brother all like to swim. _____

J. Sam and my brother have a pet turtle named Abraham who likes to swim. _____

K. Sam and Abraham want to stop swimming so they can eat. _____

L. Abraham, my pet turtle, wants to stop swimming so he can eat. _____

Answer Key

Pre/Posttest, Part 1, page 10

Name in top right corner.
1. I, 2. C, 3. C
4. A declarative sentence makes a statement.
5. An imperative sentence gives a command or makes a request.
6. 4, 7. 2, 8. 3

Answers may vary for the following:
9. There is a lot to do at a carnival. Is there a lot to do at a carnival?
10. Does Uncle Rob love to write music?
11. snapped off the tree
12. My thirsty horse
13. My favorite <u>singer</u>/appeared in a local concert.
14. Three wealthy <u>men</u>/purchased the castle.
15. A hermit lived in a cabin in the woods.
16. Into their tent crawled the tired campers.

Four Score, page 14

Name in top right corner.
1. statement   .
2. question   ?
3. command, request   .
4. sudden, strong feeling   !
A. Our   summer.   1
B. What   had!   4
C. Please   map.   3
D. The   spot.   1
E. How   built?   2
F. Roll   window.   3
G. It   here!   4
H. When   us?   2
I. Let   you.   3
J. We   trip.   1
                    Total 24

Rewrites, page 15

Name in top left corner.
Answers may vary.
1. Was the new song a hit?
2. The singer will go on tour.
3. Does she own her own jet?
4. Are her clothes really wild?
5. Her hair is usually green.
6. Does my uncle write songs?
7. Was one recorded in a studio?
8. What has Uncle Rob sold?

9. He will become famous some day.
10. Will he let fame go to his head?

Carnival Craze, page 16

Name in top left corner.
Answers may vary.
1. There is a lot to do at a carnival. Is there a lot to do at a carnival?
2. You can find fun games and rides. Can you find fun games and rides?
3. There are also Ferris wheels, clown acts and food booths. There are Ferris wheels, clown acts and food booths, also!
4. Taffy apples are a favorite carnival food. Are taffy apples a favorite carnival food?
5. At the carnival you can meet your friends and relatives. Can you meet your friends and relatives at the carnival?
6. At most carnivals there are farm displays. Are there farm displays at most carnivals?
7. Is it fun to go to carnivals? It is fun to go to carnivals!

Subject Search, page 17

1. Tiny grasshoppers (grasshoppers)
2. The insects (insects)
3. the green creatures (creatures)
4. Three sisters (sisters)
5. the girls (girls)
6. Their entire family (family)
7. The family members (members)
8. The grateful grasshoppers (grasshoppers)
9. Answers will vary.
10. Name

The simple subject for the Optional Extra Activity is in parentheses.

Two Parts, page 20

1. The sly <u>detective</u>/solved a mystery.
2. Many <u>students</u> in my class/praised his work.
3. <u>They</u>/believed he was the best detective ever.
4. Disappearing <u>ink</u>/proved to be the secret.
(Predicates will vary on 5-10.)
5. My lovely pet <u>canary</u> sings beautifully.
6. The <u>static</u> on the telephone line interrupted our conversation.
7. Her energetic <u>grandmother</u> walks three miles every day.

TLC10180 Copyright © Teaching & Learning Company, Carthage, IL 62321-0010

8. A brilliant <u>scientist</u> made an important discovery.
9. My little baby <u>brother</u> sleeps soundly.
10. A shiny black <u>limousine</u> drove up to the gate.
11. Sentences will vary.

Inverted Insights, page 21

Name in top right corner.
1. I, 2. U, 3. U, 4. I, 5. I, 6. U,
7. In the woods lived an old man.
8. In the oak tree scampered a frisky squirrel.
9. Overhead flew dozens of geese.
10. Nearby lurked two brown bears.
11. Sentences will vary.
12. Sentences will vary.

Pre/Posttest, Part 2, pages 22-23

Name in top right corner.
1. Ireland, castles, hills, sheep
2. Chicago, Detroit, Topeka (Answers will vary.)
3. last names (Answers will vary.)
4. noun, verb
5. babies–baby, potatoes–potato
6. noun
7. verb
8. has   helped
9. should be   attending
10. was   shown
11. present tense
12. choose, chose, named, ~~crown~~
13. rarely, easily
14. softly, loudly, noisily (Answers will vary.)
15. roughly, frequently, here (Answers will vary.)
16. Answers will vary.

Find the Nouns, page 25

Name in top right corner.
1. Betsy, Ireland
2. Betsy, mom, dad, brother, turtle
3. Ireland, castles, hills, sheep
4. Betsy, family, castles
5. sheep, wool, meat
6. Dublin, capital, Ireland
7. crystal, Ireland
8. Factories, tours, people, glass
9. Betsy, school, language
10. Math, reading, science, history, subjects
11. Betsy, lunch, school
12. Friends, tag, recess
13. class, students
14. teacher
15. Betsy, visit, relatives

NVA, page 26

Answers show how words are most often used.
1. A, 2. N, 3. V, 4. N, 5. NV, 6. A, 7. V,
8. NA, 9, NV, 10. N, 11. NV, 12. V, 13. NV,
14. NA, 15. A, 16. Name

Plurals, Please! page 27

Name in top left corner.
1. mice–mouse
2. calves–calf
3. peaches–peach, cherries–cherry
4. flags–flag, countries–country
5. keys–key, leaves–leaf
6. thieves–thief, feet–foot
7. oxen–ox
8. deer–deer, moose–moose
9. shoes–shoe, sheep–sheep
10. men–man, women–woman, flowers–flower
11. babies–baby, potatoes–potato
12. wives–wife, loaves–loaf

Multiple Meanings, page 28

1. verb
2. noun
3. noun
4. verb
5. adjective
6. verb
7. noun
8. adjective
9. noun
10. verb
11. noun
12. verb
13. Answers will vary.
14. Answers will vary.
15. Name

Varied Verbs, page 29

Name in left corner.

	Helping	Main
1.	has	performed
2.	were	choosing
3.	will be	rehearsing
4.	will	memorize
5.	has	helped
6.	has been	making
7.	have been	sewing
8.	will	provide
9.	can	help
10.	will be	provided
11.	should be	attending
12.	will	surpass

Divided Phrases, page 31

Main verbs are in parentheses.
1. have (visited)
2. will (remember)
3. has (met)
4. was (shown)
5. are (waiting)
6. has (seen)
7. have (left)
8. did (take)
9. will (return)
10. can (find)
11. Answers will vary.
12. Name

Verb Choice, page 34

Name in top left corner.
Answers are shown for both parts of the activity.
1. heard   (understand)   sim̷ple   tried
2. wash   cooking   eat   (peeled)
3. bl̷ue   blown   (blew)   torn
4. (exercises)   listen   jump   alm̷ost
5. play   (sung)   appear   sing
6. choose   chose   (named)   crown
7. ride   trade   finds   (used)
8. seen   (found)   disappeared   hides
9. speaks   ~~swam~~   (run)   ~~talked~~
10. (eaten)   finish   devours   cook

From Adjective to Adverb, page 36

1. warmly
2. usually
3. really
4. surely
5. hungrily
6. firstly
7. sleepily
8. commonly
9. greedily
10. rarely
11. thirstily
12. honestly
13. easily
14. shabbily
15. bravely
Name at bottom.

Opposite Adverbs, page 36

Name in top right corner.
Here are sample answers. Students' answers will vary.
1. angrily–calmly, happily
2. quietly–loudly, noisily
3. anxiously–peacefully, calmly
4. peacefully–violently, loudly
5. carelessly–carefully, neatly
6. awkwardly–smoothly, confidently
7. politely–rudely, roughly
8. often–seldom, rarely

Pre/Posttest, Part 3, pages 40-41

Name in top right corner.
1. watermelon, lemon
2. roam
3. Their car is parked over there by the tree.
4. Who's going to tell me whose pencil this is?
5. correct
6. correct
7. noisy
8. correct
9. oust (Accept any reasonable answer.)
10. feeble (Accept any reasonable answer.)
11. tea, snow, some, storm, walk, where
12. (snowstorm), somewhere
13. E, I, L, P, R, S; rise
14. pliers
15. S, D, E, G, I, T; tie
16. diets
17. mad
18. bench
19. gloss
20. reap
21. F L A T U S R U R R F Y
22. flurry
23. turf
24. T A S B A F E R K
25. breakfast (Answers may vary. This is the longest word possible.)

Watermelon Words, page 42

1. melt
2. reel
3. lemon
4. tale
5. worm
6. wee
7. roam
8. lame
9. manor
10. meter
11. meal
12. later

Spell Check, page 44

Name in top left corner.
3. believe
4. business
5. careful
7. different
8. doesn't
12. kitchen
14. noisy
16. scissors
17. separate
19. tomorrow

All other words are correct.

Synonym Search, page 46

Name in top left corner.
These words should be circled:
1. property
2. radiate
3. raid
4. oust
5. merge
6. spotless
7. grim
8. alert
9. prevent
10. jolly
11. poor
12. feeble
13. remember
14. and 15. Answers will vary.

Compound Caper, page 47

Name in top left corner.
Here are possible answers in alphabetical order.
1. afternoon
2. aircraft
3. applesauce
4. doorbell
5. drumstick
6. earmuff
7. greenhouse
8. popcorn
9. rattlesnake
10. sidewalk
11. snowstorm
12. somewhere
13. sportswear
14. stepchild
15. tablecloth
16. teamwork
17. teaspoon
18. textbook

19. themselves
20. underground

Puzzling Pyramids, page 50

Name in top right corner.
1. I, is, sir, rise, piers, pliers
2. a, pa, tap or pat, past, strap, pastry
3. I, it, tie, tide, diets, digest
4. a, at, rat, tear, heart, thread, breadth

Bonus Activity
Here are some possible answers:
vinegar–graven, raven, vane, van, an, a
leather–lather, heart, heat, eat, at, a
predict–direct, tried, diet, die, id, I
patterns–spatter, tapers, taper, part, art, at, a

First or Last? page 51

Name in top right corner.
1. chart
2. ditch
3. point
4. salt
5. the
6. flag
7. grab
8. border
9. vent
10. help
11. nurse
12. loud
13. jigsaw
14. workout
15. minute

Letter Lines, page 53

Name in top right corner.
The letters in each word should be circled in each line. Then the second word should be written in the blank.
A. amaze, gold
B. respond, vat
C. alter, erode
D. custom, vex
E. decree, qualm
F. haste, frugal
G. grave, keen
H. loyal, zest

Spell Spot, page 54

One word using all the letters is given for each number. Students' answers will vary.

1. personal
2. feedback
3. impolite
4. slippery
5. teaspoon
6. locksmith
7. breakfast
8. quicksand
9. soundproof
10. tablecloth

Name and score at bottom of page.

Pre/Posttest, Part 4, page 56

1. crab apple
2. record (Answers may vary for 1 and 2.)
3. B
4. A
5. B
6. coil, coin, cola, cold
7. Thomas Edison, the Great Inventor
   I. Edison's Childhood
   II. Edison's Early Inventions
   III. Edison's Many Patents
8. E
9. F
10. D
11. two
12. 20-26
13. after *Coast*
14. X   2   3   ④

Name in bottom right corner.

Scavenger Hunt, page 57

Name in top right corner.
Obviously, answers will vary greatly. Here are some possibilities:

1. nationalist
2. juice
3. warm spot
4. eel, eerie
5. band
6. curling iron, curve, instead
7. set
8. white chocolate, whitecap, white-collar
9. zillion, zinc
10. flight
11. over
12. split-level
13. test
14. deduct

15. ground
16. em

Guide Game, page 58

1. B
2. D
3. C
4. A
5. D
6. A
7. B
8. D
9. C
10. A
11. D
12. A
13. C
14. B
15. C

Alphabetical Antics, page 59

1. scab
2. scald
3. scale
4. scallop
5. scalp
6. scamp
7. scamper
8. scan
9. scant
10. scanty
11. scar
12. scarce
13. scare
14. scarcely
15. scarecrow
16. scarf
17. scarlet
18. scat
19. scatter
20. scatterbrain

Book Nook, page 61

Students may be able to justify additional answers as well.

1. C
2. A
3. B
4. A, B
5. D, E
6. E
7. B, D, E
8. C
9. B
10. D
11. C, A, B*, E, D
12. Name

* A bibliography can appear in various places. Often there is one at the end of each section or chapter in the text.

Index Info, page 63

Name in top left corner.

1. 6-15, 110
2. 39-43
3. seven
4. between *Map* and *Ports*
5. 48, 67, 99, 103-104
6. 46-60
7. five
8. Commercial fishing, natural resources
9. Islands
10. Answers will vary.

Encyclopedia Enterprise, page 64

Name goes above the set of encyclopedias.
The alphabet could be divided in a few different ways. Here is one solution:

1	2	3	4	5	6	7	8
A-Bg	Bh-C	D-E	F-Gi	Gi-H	I-J	K-L	M-No

9	10	11	12	13	14	15	16
Nu-Pa	Pe-Q	R	Sa-St	Su-To	Tr-U	V-W	X-Y-Z

Outline a Sandwich, page 66

Name in top right corner.
Answers will vary. Here is a sample:
Title: Three Choices When Making Peanut
Butter Sandwiches

I. Choose your bread
 A. White
 B. Whole wheat
II. Choose your peanut butter
 A. Smooth
 B. Crunchy
III. Choose your other spread
 A. Jelly
 B. Jam
 C. Honey

Pre/Posttest, Part 6, page 79

1. Listen
2. 20
3. *the*
4. Name

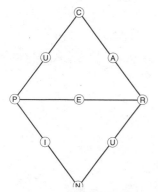

pin   cup
per   run
car

Effect	Cause
5. children have a rash	they played in poison ivy
6. letter was returned	not enough stamps

7. careless _____; roomy and spacious *capacious*; a piece of floating sea ice *floe*
8. A. ROAD
   B. ROAKD
   C. BROAKD
   D. BROAOKD
   E. BOOK
9. Sam, my brother Abraham is hungry. B
   Abraham, my brother Sam is hungry. (blank)
   Abraham, tell Sam that my brother is hungry. A

Secret Codes, page 80

Code 1: YOU HAVE THE RIGHT IDEA.
Code 2: GO BACK TWO SPACES.
Code 3: MAKE A NEW MESSAGE OF YOUR OWN.

Listening for Lists, page 81

1. atlas, encyclopedia, dictionary, almanac, etc. Answers will vary.
2. *The Top 10 of Everything 1998*
3. Cat
4. Two of these: Labrador Retriever, Rottweiler, German Shepherd
5. Jaws
6. 20
7. *the*
8. Two of these: *e, t* and *a*
9. Ireland
10. Iceland
11. spaghetti
12. Name

Diamond Diagram, page 83

Name in top left corner.

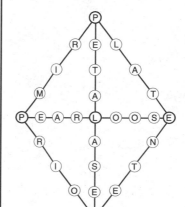

loose   laser
petal   primp
prior   pearl
enter   plate

Pause for a Cause, page 84

2. itching and swelling improved
3. children will avoid poison ivy
4. couldn't write to pen pal
5. I could write to her
6. letter was returned
7. ball game was cancelled
8. team was disappointed
9. crisp cereal
10. soft cereal

C
1. playing in poison ivy
2. used a special cream
3. rash was uncomfortable
4. lost her address
5. she wrote to me
6. not enough stamps
7. wet weather
8. had been looking forward to game
9. eat it right away
10. lets it soak in milk

Captain Jack, page 86

Name in top right corner.
1. detrimental
2. menial
3. lumbago
4. glutton
5. capacious
6. pompous
7. floe
8. collective
9. girth
10. imploring
11. haphazard
picture of Captain Jack

Soldier Salute, page 87

1. QUIETSOLDIER
2. QUILETSOLDIER
3. QUILETSOLDIET
4. QUILETSONDIET
5. QUILETSONDIGHET
6. QUILETSNDIGHET
7. QUILETKNDIGHET
8. QUILENTKNDIGHET

9. QUILENTKNIGHT
10. SILENTKNIGHT
11. SILENT KNIGHT
Name at bottom of page

Turtle Tales, page 89

Name in top right corner.
A. 6
B. extra
C. 5
D. 2
E. 1
F. 7
G. 3
H. extra
I. 4
J. extra
K. 8
L. 9